50 Summer BBQ Recipes for Home

By: Kelly Johnson

Table of Contents

- Grilled Chicken Skewers
- Barbecue Ribs
- Grilled Corn on the Cob
- Hamburgers
- Hot Dogs with Homemade Relish
- Grilled Shrimp
- Pulled Pork Sandwiches
- Grilled Veggie Platter
- BBQ Chicken Wings
- Grilled Steak with Chimichurri Sauce
- Grilled Portobello Mushrooms
- Watermelon Salad
- BBQ Baked Beans
- Potato Salad
- Coleslaw
- Grilled Fish Tacos
- BBQ Pulled Jackfruit (vegan option)
- Grilled Pineapple Dessert
- BBQ Chicken Salad
- Grilled Bratwurst with Sauerkraut
- BBQ Glazed Meatloaf
- Grilled Asparagus
- BBQ Beef Kabobs
- Grilled Peaches with Ice Cream
- BBQ Pork Belly
- Grilled Halloumi Cheese
- BBQ Chicken Skewers with Bacon
- Grilled Lobster Tails
- BBQ Stuffed Bell Peppers
- Grilled Lamb Chops
- BBQ Tofu
- Grilled Avocado
- BBQ Spare Ribs
- Grilled Caesar Salad
- BBQ Turkey Burgers

- Grilled Oysters
- BBQ Pulled Chicken
- Grilled Sweet Potatoes
- BBQ Brisket
- Grilled Eggplant Parmesan
- BBQ Salmon
- Grilled Sausage and Peppers
- BBQ Pork Chops
- Grilled Caesar Salad
- BBQ Chicken Quesadillas
- Grilled Ratatouille
- BBQ Beef Brisket Sandwiches
- Grilled Fajitas
- BBQ Stuffed Zucchini Boats
- Grilled Banana S'mores

Grilled Chicken Skewers

Ingredients:

- 4 boneless, skinless chicken breasts, cut into bite-sized pieces
- 2 bell peppers (any color), cut into chunks
- 1 large red onion, cut into chunks
- 1 zucchini, cut into rounds
- 1 cup cherry tomatoes
- Wooden or metal skewers

Marinade:

- 1/4 cup olive oil
- 3 tablespoons soy sauce
- 2 tablespoons lemon juice
- 2 tablespoons honey
- 3 cloves garlic, minced
- 1 teaspoon smoked paprika
- 1 teaspoon dried oregano
- 1 teaspoon salt
- 1/2 teaspoon black pepper

Instructions:

1. Prepare the Marinade:
   - In a medium bowl, whisk together the olive oil, soy sauce, lemon juice, honey, minced garlic, smoked paprika, dried oregano, salt, and black pepper.
2. Marinate the Chicken:
   - Place the chicken pieces in a large resealable plastic bag or a bowl.
   - Pour the marinade over the chicken, ensuring all pieces are well coated.
   - Seal the bag or cover the bowl and refrigerate for at least 30 minutes, preferably 2-4 hours for better flavor.
3. Prepare the Skewers:
   - If using wooden skewers, soak them in water for at least 30 minutes to prevent burning.
   - Thread the marinated chicken, bell peppers, red onion, zucchini, and cherry tomatoes onto the skewers, alternating between the different ingredients.
4. Preheat the Grill:
   - Preheat your grill to medium-high heat.
5. Grill the Skewers:
   - Place the skewers on the preheated grill.
   - Grill for about 10-15 minutes, turning occasionally, until the chicken is fully cooked and has nice grill marks. The internal temperature of the chicken should reach 165°F (74°C).

6. Serve:
    - Remove the skewers from the grill and let them rest for a few minutes.
    - Serve hot with your favorite side dishes, such as rice, salad, or grilled vegetables.

Enjoy your delicious grilled chicken skewers!

Barbecue Ribs

Ingredients:

- 2 racks of baby back ribs (about 4-5 pounds total)
- 1/4 cup yellow mustard

Dry Rub:

- 1/4 cup brown sugar
- 2 tablespoons paprika
- 1 tablespoon black pepper
- 1 tablespoon salt
- 1 tablespoon chili powder
- 1 tablespoon garlic powder
- 1 tablespoon onion powder
- 1 teaspoon cayenne pepper (optional for heat)

Barbecue Sauce:

- 2 cups ketchup
- 1/2 cup apple cider vinegar
- 1/4 cup brown sugar
- 2 tablespoons molasses
- 1 tablespoon Worcestershire sauce
- 1 tablespoon mustard
- 1 teaspoon smoked paprika
- 1/2 teaspoon garlic powder
- 1/2 teaspoon onion powder
- Salt and pepper to taste

Instructions:

1. Prepare the Ribs:
    - Remove the membrane from the back of the ribs. Slide a knife under the membrane and pull it off. Use a paper towel to grip it if it's slippery.
2. Apply the Mustard and Dry Rub:
    - Rub the yellow mustard all over the ribs. This helps the dry rub stick.
    - In a small bowl, mix together the brown sugar, paprika, black pepper, salt, chili powder, garlic powder, onion powder, and cayenne pepper (if using).
    - Generously coat both sides of the ribs with the dry rub, pressing it into the meat.
3. Prepare the Grill:
    - Preheat your grill to 225°F (107°C) for indirect cooking. If using a charcoal grill, push the coals to one side. If using a gas grill, turn off one burner.
4. Cook the Ribs:

- Place the ribs on the cooler side of the grill (indirect heat), bone side down.
- Close the lid and cook the ribs for 2.5 to 3 hours, maintaining a temperature of 225°F (107°C).

5. Prepare the Barbecue Sauce:
    - While the ribs are cooking, combine the ketchup, apple cider vinegar, brown sugar, molasses, Worcestershire sauce, mustard, smoked paprika, garlic powder, onion powder, salt, and pepper in a saucepan.
    - Bring to a simmer over medium heat and cook for about 10-15 minutes, stirring occasionally. Remove from heat and set aside.
6. Wrap the Ribs:
    - After 2.5 to 3 hours, remove the ribs from the grill.
    - Place each rack of ribs on a large sheet of aluminum foil. Brush both sides generously with the barbecue sauce.
    - Wrap the ribs tightly in the foil and return to the grill.
7. Finish Cooking:
    - Cook the wrapped ribs for an additional 1.5 to 2 hours, until the meat is tender and pulls away from the bones easily.
8. Caramelize the Sauce:
    - Carefully unwrap the ribs and place them back on the grill.
    - Brush more barbecue sauce on the ribs and cook for an additional 10-15 minutes over direct heat, turning occasionally, to caramelize the sauce.
9. Serve:
    - Remove the ribs from the grill and let them rest for a few minutes.
    - Slice between the bones to separate the ribs.
    - Serve with extra barbecue sauce on the side.

Enjoy your succulent barbecue ribs!

Grilled Corn on the Cob

Ingredients:

- 6 ears of corn, husks and silk removed
- 1/4 cup melted butter (or olive oil for a lighter option)
- Salt to taste
- Freshly ground black pepper to taste
- Optional toppings: chopped fresh herbs (such as cilantro or parsley), grated Parmesan cheese, lime wedges, chili powder, or smoked paprika

Instructions:

1. Prepare the Corn:
   - Preheat your grill to medium-high heat (about 375-450°F or 190-230°C).
   - If you prefer, you can soak the corn in cold water for 15-20 minutes before grilling to add moisture and prevent burning. This step is optional but recommended if you're grilling with the husks on.
2. Grill the Corn:
   - Place the ears of corn directly on the grill grates.
   - Close the grill lid and cook for about 10-15 minutes, turning every 2-3 minutes, until the corn is tender and has char marks. If grilling with the husks on, they will turn brown and slightly charred, which is fine.
3. Butter and Season:
   - Remove the corn from the grill.
   - Brush each ear with melted butter (or olive oil) while it's still hot.
   - Season with salt and freshly ground black pepper to taste.
4. Optional Toppings:
   - For extra flavor, sprinkle with chopped fresh herbs, grated Parmesan cheese, a squeeze of lime juice, or a dash of chili powder or smoked paprika.
5. Serve:
   - Serve the grilled corn on the cob hot, as a side dish to your favorite grilled meats and vegetables.

Enjoy your delicious grilled corn on the cob!

Hamburgers

Ingredients:

- 2 pounds ground beef (80% lean, 20% fat for juicier burgers)
- 1 teaspoon salt
- 1/2 teaspoon black pepper
- 1 teaspoon garlic powder
- 1 teaspoon onion powder
- 1 tablespoon Worcestershire sauce
- 4-6 hamburger buns

Optional Toppings:

- Cheese slices (cheddar, American, Swiss, etc.)
- Lettuce
- Tomato slices
- Red onion slices
- Pickles
- Ketchup
- Mustard
- Mayonnaise
- Bacon

Instructions:

1. Prepare the Patties:
   - In a large bowl, combine the ground beef, salt, black pepper, garlic powder, onion powder, and Worcestershire sauce. Mix gently until just combined; over-mixing can make the burgers tough.
   - Divide the mixture into 4-6 equal portions and shape each portion into a patty about 3/4-inch thick. Make a slight indentation in the center of each patty with your thumb to prevent the burgers from puffing up while cooking.
2. Preheat the Grill:
   - Preheat your grill to medium-high heat (about 375-400°F or 190-205°C).
3. Grill the Burgers:
   - Place the patties on the grill and cook for about 4-5 minutes on the first side, without pressing down on them.
   - Flip the burgers and cook for an additional 4-5 minutes on the second side, or until they reach your desired level of doneness (internal temperature of 160°F for well-done).
4. Add Cheese (if using):
   - If you're making cheeseburgers, add a slice of cheese to each patty during the last minute of grilling. Close the grill lid to melt the cheese.
5. Toast the Buns:

- During the last couple of minutes of grilling, place the hamburger buns cut-side down on the grill to toast lightly.
6. Assemble the Burgers:
    - Place the cooked patties on the bottom halves of the toasted buns.
    - Add your favorite toppings such as lettuce, tomato slices, red onion slices, and pickles.
    - Spread ketchup, mustard, mayonnaise, or any other desired condiments on the top halves of the buns.
    - Cover the burgers with the top halves of the buns.
7. Serve:
    - Serve the hamburgers hot with sides like French fries, potato salad, or coleslaw.

Enjoy your classic grilled hamburgers!

Hot Dogs with Homemade Relish

Ingredients:

- 8 hot dogs
- 8 hot dog buns

Homemade Relish:

- 1 cup finely chopped cucumber (seeds removed)
- 1/2 cup finely chopped red bell pepper
- 1/2 cup finely chopped green bell pepper
- 1/4 cup finely chopped red onion
- 2 tablespoons sugar
- 1/4 cup apple cider vinegar
- 1 tablespoon yellow mustard seeds
- 1/2 teaspoon salt
- 1/4 teaspoon black pepper

Instructions:

1. Prepare the Homemade Relish:
    - In a medium bowl, combine the finely chopped cucumber, red bell pepper, green bell pepper, and red onion.
    - In a small saucepan, combine the sugar, apple cider vinegar, mustard seeds, salt, and black pepper. Bring to a simmer over medium heat, stirring until the sugar is dissolved.
    - Pour the vinegar mixture over the chopped vegetables. Mix well to combine.
    - Cover and refrigerate the relish for at least 1 hour to allow the flavors to meld. For best results, prepare it a day in advance.
2. Grill the Hot Dogs:
    - Preheat your grill to medium-high heat (about 375-400°F or 190-205°C).
    - Place the hot dogs on the grill and cook, turning occasionally, until they are heated through and have nice grill marks, about 5-7 minutes.
3. Toast the Buns:
    - During the last couple of minutes of grilling, place the hot dog buns cut-side down on the grill to toast lightly.
4. Assemble the Hot Dogs:
    - Place a grilled hot dog in each toasted bun.
    - Top each hot dog with a generous spoonful of homemade relish.
5. Optional Toppings:
    - Add additional toppings as desired, such as ketchup, mustard, chopped onions, shredded cheese, sauerkraut, or jalapeños.
6. Serve:

- Serve the hot dogs hot with your favorite sides like chips, coleslaw, or potato salad.

Enjoy your delicious hot dogs with homemade relish!

Grilled Shrimp

Ingredients:

- 1 pound large shrimp, peeled and deveined (tails on or off, based on preference)
- 3 tablespoons olive oil
- 3 cloves garlic, minced
- 1 tablespoon lemon juice
- 1 teaspoon smoked paprika
- 1/2 teaspoon salt
- 1/4 teaspoon black pepper
- 1/4 teaspoon red pepper flakes (optional, for heat)
- 2 tablespoons chopped fresh parsley
- Lemon wedges, for serving
- Wooden or metal skewers

Instructions:

1. Prepare the Shrimp:
    - If using wooden skewers, soak them in water for at least 30 minutes to prevent burning.
    - Rinse the shrimp under cold water and pat dry with paper towels.
2. Marinate the Shrimp:
    - In a large bowl, whisk together the olive oil, minced garlic, lemon juice, smoked paprika, salt, black pepper, and red pepper flakes (if using).
    - Add the shrimp to the bowl and toss to coat them evenly with the marinade.
    - Cover and refrigerate for 15-30 minutes to let the flavors meld.
3. Preheat the Grill:
    - Preheat your grill to medium-high heat (about 375-400°F or 190-205°C).
4. Thread the Shrimp:
    - Thread the marinated shrimp onto the skewers, leaving a little space between each shrimp for even cooking.
5. Grill the Shrimp:
    - Place the skewers on the preheated grill.
    - Grill for about 2-3 minutes per side, until the shrimp are opaque and have nice grill marks. Be careful not to overcook, as shrimp cook quickly.
6. Serve:
    - Remove the shrimp from the grill and transfer to a serving platter.
    - Sprinkle with chopped fresh parsley and serve with lemon wedges on the side.
7. Optional Serving Suggestions:
    - Serve the grilled shrimp over a bed of rice, with a side of grilled vegetables, or in a salad.

Enjoy your delicious grilled shrimp!

Pulled Pork Sandwiches

Ingredients:

For the Pulled Pork:

- 4-5 pounds pork shoulder (also known as pork butt), boneless
- 2 tablespoons brown sugar
- 1 tablespoon smoked paprika
- 1 tablespoon garlic powder
- 1 tablespoon onion powder
- 1 tablespoon chili powder
- 1 tablespoon salt
- 1 teaspoon black pepper
- 1 cup chicken broth or apple juice
- 1 cup barbecue sauce (plus extra for serving)

For Serving:

- Hamburger buns or sandwich rolls
- Coleslaw (optional, for topping)

Instructions:

1. Prepare the Pork Shoulder:
    - In a small bowl, mix together the brown sugar, smoked paprika, garlic powder, onion powder, chili powder, salt, and black pepper to create a dry rub.
    - Rub the dry rub mixture all over the pork shoulder, covering it thoroughly.
2. Cook the Pork Shoulder:
    - Option 1: Slow Cooker Method
        - Place the seasoned pork shoulder in the slow cooker.
        - Pour the chicken broth or apple juice around the pork shoulder.
        - Cook on low for 8-10 hours or on high for 5-6 hours, until the pork is very tender and easily pulls apart with a fork.
    - Option 2: Oven Method
        - Preheat your oven to 300°F (150°C).
        - Place the seasoned pork shoulder in a roasting pan or Dutch oven.
        - Pour the chicken broth or apple juice around the pork shoulder.
        - Cover tightly with foil or a lid and roast in the oven for about 4-5 hours, until the pork is very tender and easily pulls apart with a fork.
3. Shred the Pork:
    - Once the pork is cooked and tender, remove it from the slow cooker or oven.
    - Use two forks to shred the pork into bite-sized pieces. Discard any large pieces of fat.
    - Place the shredded pork in a large bowl.

4. Add Barbecue Sauce:
    - Pour the barbecue sauce over the shredded pork.
    - Mix well to coat the pork evenly with the sauce.
    - Adjust the amount of barbecue sauce to your liking, depending on how saucy you want your pulled pork.
5. Assemble the Sandwiches:
    - Toast the hamburger buns or sandwich rolls if desired.
    - Spoon a generous amount of pulled pork onto the bottom half of each bun.
    - Optionally, top with coleslaw for added crunch and flavor.
    - Place the top half of the bun on top of the pulled pork.
6. Serve:
    - Serve the pulled pork sandwiches immediately while warm.
    - You can serve extra barbecue sauce on the side for those who want to add more.

Enjoy your delicious pulled pork sandwiches! They pair wonderfully with pickles, potato salad, or baked beans as sides.

Grilled Veggie Platter

Ingredients:

- Vegetables (choose a variety):
    - Zucchini, sliced lengthwise
    - Yellow squash, sliced lengthwise
    - Bell peppers (red, yellow, green), quartered or sliced into strips
    - Eggplant, sliced into rounds
    - Red onion, sliced into rounds or wedges
    - Asparagus spears
    - Cherry tomatoes (can be grilled on skewers or in a grilling basket)
    - Mushrooms, whole or halved (button mushrooms or portobello mushrooms)
    - Any other favorite vegetables suitable for grilling
- Marinade or Seasoning (optional):
    - 1/4 cup olive oil
    - 2-3 cloves garlic, minced
    - 1 tablespoon balsamic vinegar
    - 1 teaspoon dried herbs (such as thyme, oregano, or Italian seasoning)
    - Salt and pepper to taste
- Additional Options:
    - Fresh herbs for garnish (such as parsley, basil, or cilantro)
    - Lemon wedges, for serving
    - Balsamic glaze or drizzle (optional)

Instructions:

1. Prepare the Vegetables:
    - Preheat your grill to medium-high heat.
2. Prepare the Marinade (if using):
    - In a small bowl, whisk together the olive oil, minced garlic, balsamic vinegar, dried herbs, salt, and pepper.
3. Grill the Vegetables:
    - Place the prepared vegetables on a large baking sheet or in a large bowl.
    - If using the marinade, drizzle it over the vegetables and toss gently to coat evenly.
    - Place the vegetables directly on the grill grates or use a grilling basket or skewers for smaller vegetables like cherry tomatoes or mushrooms.
    - Grill the vegetables until they are tender and have grill marks, turning occasionally. Cooking times will vary depending on the vegetable:
        - Zucchini, yellow squash, bell peppers, and eggplant: 3-5 minutes per side.
        - Asparagus: 2-3 minutes per side.
        - Cherry tomatoes and mushrooms: 5-7 minutes, turning occasionally.

- Adjust cooking times as needed and remove vegetables from the grill as they become tender.
4. Assemble the Platter:
    - Arrange the grilled vegetables on a large platter or serving dish.
    - Garnish with fresh herbs if desired.
    - Serve with lemon wedges and a drizzle of balsamic glaze, if using.
5. Serve:
    - Serve the grilled vegetable platter warm or at room temperature as a delicious side dish or appetizer.

Enjoy your vibrant and flavorful grilled vegetable platter! It's a great complement to any meal and offers a variety of textures and flavors.

BBQ Chicken Wings

Ingredients:

- 2 pounds chicken wings, split into wingettes and drumettes
- 1 cup barbecue sauce (homemade or store-bought)
- 2 tablespoons olive oil
- 1 teaspoon garlic powder
- 1 teaspoon onion powder
- 1/2 teaspoon smoked paprika
- 1/2 teaspoon salt
- 1/4 teaspoon black pepper
- Optional: chopped fresh parsley or cilantro for garnish

Instructions:

1. Prepare the Chicken Wings:
    - In a large bowl, combine the olive oil, garlic powder, onion powder, smoked paprika, salt, and black pepper.
    - Add the chicken wings to the bowl and toss to coat evenly with the seasoning mixture.
2. Marinate the Chicken Wings:
    - Cover the bowl with plastic wrap or transfer the wings to a large resealable plastic bag.
    - Marinate in the refrigerator for at least 1 hour, or preferably up to 4 hours, to allow the flavors to meld.
3. Preheat the Grill:
    - Preheat your grill to medium-high heat (about 375-400°F or 190-205°C).
4. Grill the Chicken Wings:
    - Place the chicken wings on the preheated grill.
    - Grill for about 15-20 minutes, turning occasionally, until the wings are cooked through and have nice grill marks. The internal temperature should reach 165°F (74°C).
5. Apply BBQ Sauce:
    - During the last 5-10 minutes of grilling, brush the chicken wings generously with barbecue sauce.
    - Flip the wings and brush the other side with more barbecue sauce.
    - Continue grilling for a few more minutes to caramelize the sauce and develop flavor.
6. Serve:
    - Remove the grilled BBQ chicken wings from the grill and transfer to a serving platter.
    - Garnish with chopped fresh parsley or cilantro, if desired.
    - Serve hot with extra barbecue sauce on the side for dipping.

Enjoy your delicious BBQ chicken wings as an appetizer, main dish, or party snack! They pair perfectly with coleslaw, potato salad, or grilled vegetables.

Grilled Steak with Chimichurri Sauce

Ingredients:

For the Steak:

- 2 pounds steak of your choice (ribeye, strip loin, flank steak, or sirloin)
- Salt and pepper to taste
- Olive oil, for brushing

For the Chimichurri Sauce:

- 1 cup fresh parsley leaves, packed
- 1 cup fresh cilantro leaves, packed (optional)
- 4 cloves garlic, minced
- 1/4 cup red wine vinegar
- 1/2 cup olive oil
- 1 tablespoon fresh oregano leaves (or 1 teaspoon dried oregano)
- 1/2 teaspoon red pepper flakes (adjust to taste)
- Salt and pepper to taste

Instructions:

1. Prepare the Chimichurri Sauce:
   - In a food processor or blender, combine the parsley, cilantro (if using), minced garlic, red wine vinegar, olive oil, oregano, red pepper flakes, salt, and pepper.
   - Pulse until the herbs are finely chopped and the mixture is well combined. Alternatively, you can finely chop the parsley, cilantro, and garlic by hand and mix with the other ingredients in a bowl.
2. Season the Steak:
   - Season the steak generously with salt and pepper on both sides.
   - Brush both sides of the steak with olive oil.
3. Preheat the Grill:
   - Preheat your grill to high heat (about 450-500°F or 230-260°C).
4. Grill the Steak:
   - Place the steak on the preheated grill.
   - Grill the steak to your desired doneness, flipping once:
     - Medium rare: 3-4 minutes per side (internal temperature 130-135°F)
     - Medium: 4-5 minutes per side (internal temperature 135-145°F)
     - Medium well: 5-6 minutes per side (internal temperature 145-155°F)
     - Well done: 6-7 minutes per side (internal temperature 155°F and above)
5. Rest the Steak:
   - Remove the steak from the grill and let it rest for 5-10 minutes to allow the juices to redistribute.
6. Serve:

- Slice the steak against the grain and arrange on a serving platter.
- Spoon the chimichurri sauce generously over the sliced steak.
- Serve with additional chimichurri sauce on the side.

Optional Side Dishes:

- Grilled vegetables (such as asparagus, bell peppers, or zucchini)
- Roasted potatoes or mashed potatoes
- A fresh salad

Enjoy your delicious grilled steak with chimichurri sauce!

Grilled Portobello Mushrooms

Ingredients:

- 4 large portobello mushrooms
- 1/4 cup olive oil
- 3 tablespoons balsamic vinegar
- 2 cloves garlic, minced
- 1 teaspoon dried thyme or fresh thyme leaves
- Salt and pepper to taste
- Optional toppings: chopped fresh parsley, grated Parmesan cheese, or crumbled goat cheese

Instructions:

1. Prepare the Mushrooms:
    - Gently clean the portobello mushrooms with a damp paper towel to remove any dirt. Remove the stems and, if desired, use a spoon to scrape out the gills (this step is optional, but removing the gills can prevent the mushrooms from becoming too dark and muddy-looking when cooked).
2. Make the Marinade:
    - In a small bowl, whisk together the olive oil, balsamic vinegar, minced garlic, thyme, salt, and pepper.
3. Marinate the Mushrooms:
    - Place the mushrooms in a large resealable plastic bag or a shallow dish.
    - Pour the marinade over the mushrooms, ensuring they are well-coated.
    - Let the mushrooms marinate for at least 15-30 minutes, turning occasionally to ensure even marination.
4. Preheat the Grill:
    - Preheat your grill to medium-high heat (about 375-400°F or 190-205°C).
5. Grill the Mushrooms:
    - Remove the mushrooms from the marinade and shake off any excess.
    - Place the mushrooms on the preheated grill, gill side down.
    - Grill for about 5-7 minutes per side, until the mushrooms are tender and have nice grill marks. Baste with any remaining marinade during grilling if desired.
6. Serve:
    - Remove the mushrooms from the grill and transfer to a serving platter.
    - Optionally, sprinkle with chopped fresh parsley, grated Parmesan cheese, or crumbled goat cheese for added flavor.
    - Serve the grilled portobello mushrooms as a main dish, in a sandwich, or as a side to your favorite grilled meats or salads.

Enjoy your delicious and hearty grilled portobello mushrooms!

Watermelon Salad

Ingredients:

- 4 cups watermelon, cut into bite-sized cubes
- 1 cup cucumber, diced
- 1/2 cup red onion, thinly sliced
- 1/2 cup feta cheese, crumbled
- 1/4 cup fresh mint leaves, chopped
- 1/4 cup fresh basil leaves, chopped

For the Dressing:

- 2 tablespoons olive oil
- 1 tablespoon fresh lime juice
- 1 teaspoon honey or agave syrup
- Salt and pepper to taste

Instructions:

1. Prepare the Salad Ingredients:
   - In a large bowl, combine the watermelon cubes, diced cucumber, thinly sliced red onion, crumbled feta cheese, chopped mint, and chopped basil.
2. Make the Dressing:
   - In a small bowl, whisk together the olive oil, fresh lime juice, honey (or agave syrup), salt, and pepper until well combined.
3. Assemble the Salad:
   - Pour the dressing over the salad ingredients.
   - Gently toss the salad to ensure all the ingredients are evenly coated with the dressing.
4. Serve:
   - Transfer the salad to a serving bowl or platter.
   - Serve immediately for the best flavor and texture.

Optional Additions:

- Avocado: Add diced avocado for a creamy texture.
- Nuts or Seeds: Sprinkle with toasted pine nuts, sunflower seeds, or chopped walnuts for extra crunch.
- Berries: Add fresh blueberries or raspberries for an extra burst of flavor.

Enjoy your refreshing watermelon salad! It's perfect as a light appetizer, side dish, or even a healthy dessert.

BBQ Baked Beans

Ingredients:

- 4 slices bacon, chopped
- 1 small onion, diced
- 1 small green bell pepper, diced
- 3 cloves garlic, minced
- 3 cans (15 ounces each) navy beans or pinto beans, drained and rinsed
- 1 cup barbecue sauce
- 1/2 cup ketchup
- 1/4 cup molasses
- 1/4 cup brown sugar
- 2 tablespoons yellow mustard
- 1 tablespoon Worcestershire sauce
- 1 teaspoon smoked paprika
- 1/2 teaspoon salt
- 1/2 teaspoon black pepper

Instructions:

1. Preheat the Oven:
   - Preheat your oven to 350°F (175°C).
2. Cook the Bacon:
   - In a large skillet over medium heat, cook the chopped bacon until it is crisp and browned.
   - Use a slotted spoon to transfer the cooked bacon to a paper towel-lined plate to drain. Leave about 1 tablespoon of bacon grease in the skillet.
3. Sauté the Vegetables:
   - Add the diced onion and green bell pepper to the skillet with the bacon grease.
   - Sauté for about 5 minutes, until the vegetables are softened.
   - Add the minced garlic and cook for an additional 1-2 minutes, until fragrant.
4. Mix the Beans:
   - In a large bowl, combine the drained and rinsed beans, cooked bacon, sautéed vegetables, barbecue sauce, ketchup, molasses, brown sugar, yellow mustard, Worcestershire sauce, smoked paprika, salt, and black pepper.
   - Stir well to combine all the ingredients.
5. Bake the Beans:
   - Transfer the bean mixture to a 9x13-inch baking dish.
   - Cover the dish with aluminum foil and bake in the preheated oven for 45 minutes.
   - Remove the foil and bake for an additional 15-20 minutes, until the sauce is thickened and bubbly.
6. Serve:

- - Remove the baked beans from the oven and let them cool for a few minutes before serving.

Enjoy your delicious BBQ baked beans as a side dish for your favorite grilled meats, burgers, or hot dogs. They also pair wonderfully with cornbread and coleslaw!

Potato Salad

Ingredients:

- 2 pounds potatoes (Yukon gold or red potatoes are great choices)
- 3 large eggs
- 1 cup mayonnaise
- 1/4 cup Dijon mustard
- 2 tablespoons apple cider vinegar
- 1 tablespoon sugar
- 1 teaspoon salt
- 1/2 teaspoon black pepper
- 1/2 teaspoon celery seed (optional)
- 1/2 cup finely chopped red onion
- 1/2 cup finely chopped celery
- 1/4 cup chopped pickles or relish (optional)
- 1/4 cup chopped fresh parsley (optional)

Instructions:

1. Cook the Potatoes:
    - Wash and peel the potatoes (you can leave the skin on if using thin-skinned potatoes like red potatoes).
    - Cut the potatoes into bite-sized cubes.
    - Place the potatoes in a large pot and cover with cold water. Add a pinch of salt.
    - Bring to a boil, then reduce the heat and simmer for about 10-15 minutes, or until the potatoes are tender but not falling apart.
    - Drain the potatoes and let them cool slightly.
2. Cook the Eggs:
    - While the potatoes are cooking, place the eggs in a small pot and cover with water.
    - Bring to a boil, then reduce the heat to low and simmer for 10 minutes.
    - Drain the hot water and fill the pot with cold water and ice to cool the eggs quickly.
    - Once cooled, peel the eggs and chop them.
3. Prepare the Dressing:
    - In a large bowl, whisk together the mayonnaise, Dijon mustard, apple cider vinegar, sugar, salt, black pepper, and celery seed (if using).
4. Combine the Salad:
    - Add the cooked and slightly cooled potatoes to the bowl with the dressing.
    - Add the chopped eggs, finely chopped red onion, celery, pickles or relish (if using), and fresh parsley (if using).
    - Gently fold the ingredients together until everything is well coated with the dressing.

5. Chill the Salad:
    - Cover the bowl and refrigerate the potato salad for at least 1 hour to allow the flavors to meld. For the best flavor, refrigerate for several hours or overnight.
6. Serve:
    - Serve the potato salad chilled, garnished with extra parsley or paprika if desired.

Enjoy your creamy and delicious potato salad! It pairs perfectly with grilled meats, sandwiches, or as part of a picnic spread.

Coleslaw

Ingredients:

For the Coleslaw:

- 1 medium head green cabbage, finely shredded (about 6 cups)
- 2 large carrots, peeled and grated
- 1/2 red onion, thinly sliced (optional)
- 1/4 cup fresh parsley, chopped (optional)

For the Dressing:

- 1 cup mayonnaise
- 1/4 cup apple cider vinegar
- 2 tablespoons Dijon mustard
- 2 tablespoons sugar
- 1 teaspoon celery seed (optional)
- 1/2 teaspoon salt
- 1/4 teaspoon black pepper

Instructions:

1. Prepare the Vegetables:
    - Remove the outer leaves from the cabbage and cut it into quarters.
    - Remove the core from each quarter and finely shred the cabbage using a knife, mandoline, or food processor.
    - Peel and grate the carrots.
    - Thinly slice the red onion, if using.
    - Chop the parsley, if using.
2. Make the Dressing:
    - In a large bowl, whisk together the mayonnaise, apple cider vinegar, Dijon mustard, sugar, celery seed (if using), salt, and black pepper until well combined.
3. Combine the Salad:
    - Add the shredded cabbage, grated carrots, and sliced red onion (if using) to the bowl with the dressing.
    - Toss everything together until the vegetables are evenly coated with the dressing.
    - Stir in the chopped parsley, if using.
4. Chill the Coleslaw:
    - Cover the bowl and refrigerate the coleslaw for at least 1 hour before serving to allow the flavors to meld. For the best flavor, refrigerate for several hours or overnight.
5. Serve:
    - Serve the coleslaw chilled as a side dish.

Optional Variations:

- Creamy Variation: Add 1/4 cup sour cream or Greek yogurt to the dressing for extra creaminess.
- Tangy Variation: Add a squeeze of fresh lemon juice to the dressing for extra tang.
- Sweet Variation: Add 1/4 cup raisins or dried cranberries for a sweet contrast.

Enjoy your delicious and refreshing coleslaw! It's a great accompaniment to grilled meats, sandwiches, or as a topping for burgers and hot dogs.

Grilled Fish Tacos

Ingredients:

For the Fish:

- 1 1/2 pounds white fish fillets (such as tilapia, cod, or mahi-mahi)
- 2 tablespoons olive oil
- 2 tablespoons lime juice
- 2 cloves garlic, minced
- 1 teaspoon ground cumin
- 1 teaspoon chili powder
- 1/2 teaspoon smoked paprika
- Salt and pepper to taste

For the Tacos:

- Corn or flour tortillas
- 2 cups shredded cabbage (green or purple, or a mix)
- 1/2 cup fresh cilantro, chopped
- 1/2 red onion, thinly sliced
- 1 avocado, sliced
- Lime wedges, for serving

For the Lime Crema:

- 1/2 cup sour cream or Greek yogurt
- 2 tablespoons mayonnaise
- 1 tablespoon lime juice
- 1 teaspoon lime zest
- 1 clove garlic, minced
- Salt and pepper to taste

Instructions:

1. Prepare the Fish Marinade:
    - In a small bowl, mix together the olive oil, lime juice, minced garlic, ground cumin, chili powder, smoked paprika, salt, and pepper.
    - Place the fish fillets in a shallow dish or resealable plastic bag.
    - Pour the marinade over the fish, ensuring it is well-coated.
    - Marinate in the refrigerator for at least 30 minutes, or up to 1 hour.
2. Prepare the Lime Crema:
    - In a small bowl, whisk together the sour cream (or Greek yogurt), mayonnaise, lime juice, lime zest, minced garlic, salt, and pepper until smooth.
    - Cover and refrigerate until ready to use.

3. Preheat the Grill:
    - Preheat your grill to medium-high heat (about 375-400°F or 190-205°C).
4. Grill the Fish:
    - Remove the fish from the marinade and shake off any excess.
    - Place the fish on the preheated grill.
    - Grill for about 3-4 minutes per side, or until the fish is opaque and flakes easily with a fork.
    - Remove the fish from the grill and let it rest for a few minutes before flaking it into large chunks.
5. Assemble the Tacos:
    - Warm the tortillas on the grill for about 20-30 seconds per side, or until lightly charred and pliable.
    - Fill each tortilla with grilled fish.
    - Top with shredded cabbage, fresh cilantro, sliced red onion, and avocado slices.
    - Drizzle with lime crema.
6. Serve:
    - Serve the grilled fish tacos immediately with lime wedges on the side for squeezing over the top.

Optional Toppings:

- Pico de gallo or salsa
- Pickled jalapeños
- Cotija cheese, crumbled
- Hot sauce

Enjoy your delicious and fresh grilled fish tacos! They are perfect for a light and satisfying meal.

BBQ Pulled Jackfruit (vegan option)

Ingredients:

- 2 cans young green jackfruit in water or brine (20 ounces each)
- 1 tablespoon olive oil
- 1 small onion, finely chopped
- 3 cloves garlic, minced
- 1 cup barbecue sauce (make sure it's vegan)
- 1 tablespoon soy sauce or tamari
- 1 tablespoon apple cider vinegar
- 1 teaspoon smoked paprika
- 1/2 teaspoon chili powder
- Salt and pepper to taste

Instructions:

1. Prepare the Jackfruit:
    - Drain and rinse the jackfruit thoroughly.
    - Cut off the core portion of the jackfruit pieces (the harder triangular part) and discard or set aside. This step is optional, but it helps achieve a more shredded texture.
    - Use your hands or a fork to pull apart the jackfruit pieces into shreds.
2. Cook the Jackfruit:
    - In a large skillet, heat the olive oil over medium heat.
    - Add the finely chopped onion and sauté for about 5 minutes, until it becomes translucent.
    - Add the minced garlic and cook for another minute, until fragrant.
3. Add the Jackfruit and Seasonings:
    - Add the shredded jackfruit to the skillet and stir to combine with the onions and garlic.
    - Add the barbecue sauce, soy sauce (or tamari), apple cider vinegar, smoked paprika, chili powder, salt, and pepper.
    - Stir well to ensure the jackfruit is evenly coated with the sauce and seasonings.
4. Simmer the Mixture:
    - Reduce the heat to low and cover the skillet.
    - Let the jackfruit mixture simmer for about 20-30 minutes, stirring occasionally, until the jackfruit is tender and has absorbed the flavors of the sauce.
5. Serve:
    - Serve the BBQ pulled jackfruit on sandwich buns or slider rolls.
    - Optionally, top with coleslaw, pickles, or extra barbecue sauce.

Optional Toppings and Sides:

- Toppings: Coleslaw, pickles, sliced red onion, fresh cilantro, avocado slices
- Sides: Potato salad, baked beans, corn on the cob, grilled vegetables

Enjoy your flavorful and satisfying BBQ pulled jackfruit sandwiches! They are perfect for a vegan-friendly barbecue or a tasty weeknight dinner.

Grilled Pineapple Dessert

Ingredients:

- 1 ripe pineapple
- 2 tablespoons honey or maple syrup
- 1 teaspoon ground cinnamon
- 1 tablespoon melted butter or coconut oil (optional, for extra richness)
- Vanilla ice cream or whipped cream, for serving (optional)
- Fresh mint leaves, for garnish (optional)

Instructions:

1. Prepare the Pineapple:
   - Cut off the top and bottom of the pineapple.
   - Stand the pineapple upright and slice off the skin, removing any "eyes" (small brown spots).
   - Cut the pineapple into rings or wedges, removing the core from each piece if desired.
2. Make the Glaze:
   - In a small bowl, mix together the honey (or maple syrup), ground cinnamon, and melted butter or coconut oil (if using).
3. Preheat the Grill:
   - Preheat your grill to medium-high heat (about 375-400°F or 190-205°C).
4. Grill the Pineapple:
   - Brush each piece of pineapple with the honey-cinnamon glaze.
   - Place the pineapple pieces on the preheated grill.
   - Grill for about 3-4 minutes per side, until the pineapple is caramelized and has nice grill marks.
5. Serve:
   - Remove the grilled pineapple from the grill and transfer to a serving platter.
   - Optionally, serve with a scoop of vanilla ice cream or a dollop of whipped cream.
   - Garnish with fresh mint leaves, if desired.

Optional Variations:

- Spiced Variation: Add a pinch of ground nutmeg or cloves to the honey-cinnamon glaze for extra warmth.
- Citrus Variation: Squeeze fresh lime or orange juice over the grilled pineapple before serving for a citrusy twist.
- Tropical Variation: Serve with a sprinkle of toasted coconut flakes for added texture and flavor.

Enjoy your delicious and easy grilled pineapple dessert! It's a perfect way to end a meal on a sweet and tropical note.

BBQ Chicken Salad

Ingredients:

For the BBQ Chicken:

- 2 boneless, skinless chicken breasts
- Salt and pepper to taste
- 1 cup barbecue sauce (homemade or store-bought)

For the Salad:

- 6 cups mixed salad greens (such as romaine, spinach, or spring mix)
- 1 cup cherry tomatoes, halved
- 1/2 cup corn kernels (fresh, canned, or thawed if frozen)
- 1/2 cup black beans, drained and rinsed
- 1/4 cup red onion, thinly sliced
- 1/4 cup shredded cheddar cheese (optional)
- 1 avocado, sliced

For the Dressing:

- 1/4 cup ranch dressing (homemade or store-bought)
- 2 tablespoons barbecue sauce
- 1 tablespoon lime juice
- Salt and pepper to taste

Instructions:

1. Grill the Chicken:
    - Preheat your grill to medium-high heat.
    - Season the chicken breasts with salt and pepper.
    - Grill the chicken for about 5-7 minutes per side, or until cooked through and no longer pink in the center.
    - Brush the chicken with barbecue sauce during the last few minutes of grilling, flipping once, to coat evenly.
    - Remove the chicken from the grill and let it rest for a few minutes before slicing or chopping into bite-sized pieces.
2. Prepare the Salad Ingredients:
    - In a large salad bowl, combine the mixed greens, cherry tomatoes, corn kernels, black beans, red onion, shredded cheddar cheese (if using), and sliced avocado.
3. Make the Dressing:
    - In a small bowl, whisk together the ranch dressing, barbecue sauce, lime juice, salt, and pepper until well combined.
4. Assemble the Salad:

- Add the grilled BBQ chicken pieces to the salad bowl.
- Drizzle the dressing over the salad ingredients.
- Gently toss everything together until well coated with the dressing.
5. Serve:
    - Divide the BBQ chicken salad among serving plates or bowls.
    - Garnish with additional barbecue sauce drizzle or chopped fresh cilantro, if desired.
    - Serve immediately and enjoy!

Optional Additions:

- Crunchy Toppings: Add crispy tortilla strips or crushed tortilla chips for extra texture.
- Fresh Herbs: Sprinkle with chopped fresh cilantro or parsley for added freshness.
- Diced Bell Peppers: Add diced red or green bell peppers for more color and crunch.

This BBQ chicken salad is perfect for a satisfying and wholesome meal. It's packed with flavors and textures that will satisfy your taste buds!

Grilled Bratwurst with Sauerkraut

Ingredients:

- 4 bratwurst sausages
- 4 sausage buns or hoagie rolls
- 2 cups sauerkraut, drained
- 1 tablespoon olive oil
- 1 small onion, thinly sliced
- 1 teaspoon caraway seeds (optional)
- Salt and pepper to taste
- Mustard (such as Dijon or whole grain), for serving

Instructions:

1. Prepare the Grill:
    - Preheat your grill to medium-high heat.
2. Grill the Bratwurst:
    - Place the bratwurst sausages on the preheated grill.
    - Grill for about 15-20 minutes, turning occasionally, until the sausages are cooked through and have grill marks.
3. Prepare the Sauerkraut:
    - While the bratwurst is grilling, heat olive oil in a skillet over medium heat.
    - Add the thinly sliced onion and sauté until softened and lightly caramelized, about 5-7 minutes.
    - Add the drained sauerkraut and caraway seeds (if using) to the skillet.
    - Season with salt and pepper to taste.
    - Cook for another 5-7 minutes, stirring occasionally, until the sauerkraut is heated through and flavors are combined.
4. Toast the Buns:
    - In the last few minutes of grilling the bratwurst, place the sausage buns or hoagie rolls on the grill to lightly toast.
5. Assemble the Bratwurst Sandwiches:
    - Place each grilled bratwurst sausage in a bun or hoagie roll.
    - Top each bratwurst with a generous portion of the sautéed sauerkraut and onions.
6. Serve:
    - Serve the grilled bratwurst with sauerkraut sandwiches immediately, with mustard on the side for dipping or spreading.

Optional Additions:

- Cheese: Add a slice of Swiss cheese or cheddar cheese to melt over the bratwurst.
- Pickles: Serve with dill pickles on the side for a tangy contrast.

- Potato Salad: Serve alongside potato salad for a classic German-inspired meal.

Enjoy your delicious grilled bratwurst with sauerkraut sandwiches! They are perfect for a casual and satisfying meal, especially when served with a cold beer or cider.

BBQ Glazed Meatloaf

Ingredients:

For the Meatloaf:

- 1 pound ground beef (or a mix of beef and pork)
- 1/2 cup breadcrumbs
- 1/4 cup milk
- 1 small onion, finely chopped
- 1/2 bell pepper, finely chopped
- 2 cloves garlic, minced
- 1 large egg, lightly beaten
- 1 tablespoon Worcestershire sauce
- 1 teaspoon salt
- 1/2 teaspoon black pepper
- 1/2 teaspoon dried thyme
- 1/2 teaspoon dried oregano
- 1/4 teaspoon smoked paprika (optional)
- Cooking spray or olive oil, for greasing

For the BBQ Glaze:

- 1/2 cup barbecue sauce (homemade or store-bought)
- 2 tablespoons ketchup
- 1 tablespoon brown sugar
- 1 tablespoon apple cider vinegar
- 1 teaspoon Dijon mustard

Instructions:

1. Preheat the Oven:
    - Preheat your oven to 350°F (175°C).
2. Prepare the Meatloaf Mixture:
    - In a large bowl, combine the ground beef, breadcrumbs, milk, chopped onion, chopped bell pepper, minced garlic, beaten egg, Worcestershire sauce, salt, black pepper, dried thyme, dried oregano, and smoked paprika (if using).
    - Mix everything together gently but thoroughly, using your hands or a spoon, until well combined.
3. Shape the Meatloaf:
    - Lightly grease a baking dish or loaf pan with cooking spray or olive oil.
    - Transfer the meatloaf mixture into the prepared baking dish.
    - Shape the mixture into a loaf shape, about 8 inches long and 4 inches wide.
4. Make the BBQ Glaze:

- In a small bowl, whisk together the barbecue sauce, ketchup, brown sugar, apple cider vinegar, and Dijon mustard until smooth.
5. Glaze and Bake the Meatloaf:
    - Brush or spoon half of the BBQ glaze evenly over the top of the meatloaf.
    - Reserve the remaining glaze for later.
    - Bake the meatloaf in the preheated oven for 45 minutes to 1 hour, or until cooked through. The internal temperature should reach 160°F (71°C) for ground beef.
6. Apply the Remaining Glaze:
    - During the last 15 minutes of baking, brush the remaining BBQ glaze over the top of the meatloaf.
    - Continue baking until the glaze is sticky and caramelized.
7. Rest and Serve:
    - Remove the meatloaf from the oven and let it rest for 10 minutes before slicing.
    - Serve slices of BBQ glazed meatloaf with mashed potatoes, roasted vegetables, or a fresh salad.

Tips:

- Make sure to use lean ground beef or a mixture with a higher fat content for a juicier meatloaf.
- You can customize the meatloaf by adding diced bell peppers, carrots, or even shredded cheese to the mixture.
- Leftover meatloaf slices are great for sandwiches or as a topping for salads.

Enjoy your delicious BBQ glazed meatloaf! It's a comforting and satisfying meal that's perfect for any day of the week.

Grilled Asparagus

Ingredients:

- 1 pound fresh asparagus spears
- 2 tablespoons olive oil
- Salt and pepper to taste
- Optional: lemon wedges, grated Parmesan cheese, balsamic glaze, or toasted almonds for serving

Instructions:

1. Prepare the Asparagus:
    - Wash the asparagus spears and trim off the tough ends (about 1-2 inches from the bottom). You can snap them off where they naturally break or use a knife to trim.
2. Preheat the Grill:
    - Preheat your grill to medium-high heat. If you're using a gas grill, aim for around 400°F (about 200°C).
3. Season the Asparagus:
    - Place the trimmed asparagus spears in a large bowl.
    - Drizzle olive oil over the asparagus and toss to coat evenly.
    - Season with salt and pepper to taste. You can also add garlic powder, lemon zest, or your favorite herbs for extra flavor.
4. Grill the Asparagus:
    - Arrange the seasoned asparagus spears in a single layer on the preheated grill.
    - Grill for about 4-6 minutes, turning occasionally with tongs, until the asparagus is tender and lightly charred. The cooking time may vary depending on the thickness of the asparagus spears.
5. Serve:
    - Transfer the grilled asparagus to a serving platter.
    - Squeeze fresh lemon juice over the asparagus if desired.
    - Optionally, sprinkle with grated Parmesan cheese, drizzle with balsamic glaze, or sprinkle with toasted almonds before serving.

Tips:

- Grill Basket: If you're concerned about the asparagus falling through the grates, you can use a grill basket or grill mat to grill them more easily.
- Preparation Variations: You can also wrap the asparagus in foil packets with a drizzle of olive oil and seasonings for a different cooking method on the grill.

Grilled asparagus makes a fantastic side dish for grilled meats, seafood, or as part of a vegetarian meal. It's quick to prepare and adds a delightful touch to any barbecue or summer gathering. Enjoy!

BBQ Beef Kabobs

Ingredients:

- 1 1/2 pounds beef sirloin or top sirloin steak, cut into 1-inch cubes
- 1 large red bell pepper, cut into 1-inch pieces
- 1 large green bell pepper, cut into 1-inch pieces
- 1 large red onion, cut into 1-inch pieces
- 8-10 wooden or metal skewers

For the Marinade:

- 1/4 cup soy sauce
- 1/4 cup olive oil
- 2 tablespoons Worcestershire sauce
- 2 tablespoons honey or brown sugar
- 2 cloves garlic, minced
- 1 teaspoon smoked paprika
- 1/2 teaspoon black pepper
- 1/2 teaspoon onion powder
- 1/2 teaspoon dried thyme

For the BBQ Glaze:

- 1/2 cup barbecue sauce (homemade or store-bought)
- 2 tablespoons honey or maple syrup
- 1 tablespoon apple cider vinegar
- 1/2 teaspoon garlic powder
- Salt and pepper to taste

Instructions:

1. Prepare the Marinade:
    - In a bowl, whisk together the soy sauce, olive oil, Worcestershire sauce, honey or brown sugar, minced garlic, smoked paprika, black pepper, onion powder, and dried thyme.
2. Marinate the Beef:
    - Place the beef cubes in a shallow dish or resealable plastic bag.
    - Pour the marinade over the beef, making sure it is well coated.
    - Cover the dish or seal the bag and refrigerate for at least 1 hour, or up to 4 hours, to allow the flavors to meld.
3. Prepare the BBQ Glaze:
    - In a small saucepan, combine the barbecue sauce, honey or maple syrup, apple cider vinegar, garlic powder, salt, and pepper.

- Bring to a simmer over medium heat, stirring occasionally, and cook for 5-7 minutes until slightly thickened.
      - Remove from heat and set aside.
   4. Assemble the Kabobs:
      - Preheat your grill to medium-high heat.
      - Thread the marinated beef cubes, alternating with pieces of bell pepper and red onion, onto the skewers.
   5. Grill the Kabobs:
      - Place the assembled kabobs on the preheated grill.
      - Grill for about 8-10 minutes, turning occasionally, until the beef is cooked to your desired doneness and the vegetables are tender and slightly charred.
   6. Glaze the Kabobs:
      - During the last few minutes of grilling, brush the BBQ glaze over the kabobs, turning and brushing occasionally, until the glaze is caramelized and sticky.
   7. Serve:
      - Remove the BBQ beef kabobs from the grill and let them rest for a few minutes.
      - Serve hot, garnished with chopped fresh parsley or cilantro if desired.
      - Enjoy your delicious BBQ beef kabobs with rice, salad, or grilled vegetables on the side!

Tips:

- Vegetarian Option: Replace the beef cubes with extra firm tofu or large mushroom caps for a vegetarian option.
- Grill Preparation: Soak wooden skewers in water for at least 30 minutes before threading to prevent them from burning on the grill.

BBQ beef kabobs are a crowd-pleasing dish that's perfect for summer barbecues or any outdoor gathering. They're easy to customize with your favorite vegetables and make for a satisfying meal straight from the grill.

Grilled Peaches with Ice Cream

Ingredients:

- 4 ripe peaches, halved and pits removed
- 2 tablespoons melted butter or olive oil
- 1-2 tablespoons honey or brown sugar (optional, depending on sweetness of peaches)
- Vanilla ice cream or your favorite flavor
- Optional toppings: honey, cinnamon, chopped nuts, or fresh mint leaves

Instructions:

1. Prepare the Grill:
    - Preheat your grill to medium-high heat.
2. Prepare the Peaches:
    - Halve the peaches and remove the pits.
    - Brush the cut side of each peach half with melted butter or olive oil. If desired, drizzle a little honey or sprinkle brown sugar over each peach half for added sweetness.
3. Grill the Peaches:
    - Place the peach halves cut side down on the preheated grill.
    - Grill for about 3-4 minutes, until grill marks appear and the peaches are slightly softened.
4. Flip and Grill:
    - Carefully flip the peach halves using tongs.
    - Grill for an additional 2-3 minutes on the skin side to warm through.
5. Serve:
    - Remove the grilled peaches from the grill and let them cool slightly.
    - Place each peach half in a serving bowl or plate.
    - Top each peach half with a scoop of vanilla ice cream or your favorite ice cream flavor.
6. Optional Toppings:
    - Drizzle a little honey over the grilled peaches and ice cream.
    - Sprinkle with a pinch of cinnamon, chopped nuts (such as almonds or pecans), or garnish with fresh mint leaves.
7. Enjoy:
    - Serve immediately while the peaches are warm and the ice cream begins to melt slightly.
    - Enjoy the delicious combination of grilled peaches and creamy ice cream!

Tips:

- Variations: You can also sprinkle a little cinnamon or nutmeg on the peaches before grilling for extra flavor.

- Grill Preparation: Ensure your grill grates are clean and well-oiled to prevent sticking.

Grilled peaches with ice cream are perfect for summer evenings or outdoor gatherings. They're quick to prepare and make a beautiful and tasty dessert that's sure to impress!

BBQ Pork Belly

Ingredients:

- 2 pounds pork belly, skin removed and cut into 1-inch thick slices or cubes
- Salt and pepper to taste
- BBQ sauce (homemade or store-bought)
- Optional: chopped fresh herbs for garnish (such as parsley or cilantro)

Instructions:

1. Prepare the Pork Belly:
    - If the pork belly still has the skin on, remove it by carefully slicing it off with a sharp knife.
    - Cut the pork belly into slices or cubes, about 1 inch thick. Pat dry with paper towels to remove excess moisture.
2. Season the Pork Belly:
    - Season the pork belly pieces generously with salt and pepper on all sides.
3. Preheat the Grill:
    - Preheat your grill to medium-high heat. Aim for a temperature around 375-400°F (190-205°C).
4. Grill the Pork Belly:
    - Place the seasoned pork belly pieces on the preheated grill.
    - Grill for about 4-5 minutes per side, depending on the thickness of the slices or cubes, until the pork belly is golden brown and slightly caramelized.
5. Apply BBQ Sauce:
    - Brush BBQ sauce over the grilled pork belly pieces during the last few minutes of grilling, turning and brushing occasionally to coat evenly.
    - Continue grilling for another 1-2 minutes per side, allowing the BBQ sauce to caramelize and create a sticky glaze.
6. Serve:
    - Remove the BBQ pork belly from the grill and transfer to a serving platter.
    - Garnish with chopped fresh herbs, if desired.
    - Serve hot and enjoy immediately!

Tips:

- Temperature: Ensure the internal temperature of the pork belly reaches 145°F (63°C) for safe consumption.
- Resting: Let the grilled BBQ pork belly rest for a few minutes before serving to allow the juices to redistribute.

BBQ pork belly is a rich and flavorful dish that pairs well with a variety of sides, such as coleslaw, roasted vegetables, or grilled corn on the cob. It's sure to be a hit at any barbecue or gathering!

Grilled Halloumi Cheese

Ingredients:

- 1 block (about 8 ounces) halloumi cheese, cut into 1/2-inch thick slices
- 1-2 tablespoons olive oil, for brushing
- Freshly ground black pepper, to taste
- Optional: lemon wedges, fresh herbs (such as mint or basil) for serving

Instructions:

1. Prepare the Grill:
   - Preheat your grill to medium-high heat. If using a stovetop grill pan, preheat it over medium-high heat.
2. Prepare the Halloumi:
   - Cut the halloumi cheese into slices that are about 1/2-inch thick. Pat them dry with a paper towel to remove any excess moisture.
3. Grill the Halloumi:
   - Brush both sides of each halloumi slice lightly with olive oil. This will help prevent sticking and promote browning.
   - Place the halloumi slices on the preheated grill or grill pan.
   - Grill for about 2-3 minutes on each side, or until grill marks appear and the cheese is heated through. The cheese should be golden brown and slightly crispy on the outside while still soft and slightly gooey on the inside.
4. Serve:
   - Transfer the grilled halloumi slices to a serving platter or individual plates.
   - Sprinkle with freshly ground black pepper to taste.
   - Optionally, serve with lemon wedges for squeezing over the cheese and fresh herbs for garnish.

Serving Suggestions:

- Salads: Serve grilled halloumi on a bed of mixed greens with cherry tomatoes, cucumber slices, and a drizzle of balsamic glaze.
- Sandwiches: Use grilled halloumi slices as a delicious filling for sandwiches or burgers.
- Appetizers: Serve grilled halloumi as part of a Mediterranean-style appetizer platter with olives, roasted red peppers, and pita bread.

Grilled halloumi cheese is best enjoyed hot off the grill when it's still warm and slightly gooey inside. Its salty and slightly tangy flavor pairs beautifully with the smokiness from grilling. It's a versatile dish that can be served as an appetizer, side dish, or part of a larger meal. Enjoy!

BBQ Chicken Skewers with Bacon

Ingredients:

- 1 pound boneless, skinless chicken breasts, cut into 1-inch cubes
- 8-10 slices of bacon, cut into halves or thirds (depending on length)
- 1/2 cup barbecue sauce (homemade or store-bought)
- Wooden skewers, soaked in water for 30 minutes if using

Instructions:

1. Prepare the Chicken and Bacon:
   - Cut the chicken breasts into 1-inch cubes.
   - Cut each slice of bacon into halves or thirds, depending on the length and how much you want to wrap around each chicken cube.
2. Assemble the Skewers:
   - Thread the chicken cubes onto the wooden skewers, alternating with pieces of bacon. Wrap each chicken cube with a strip of bacon, securing the ends of the bacon onto the skewer.
3. Prepare the BBQ Sauce:
   - In a small bowl, mix the barbecue sauce until smooth.
4. Grill the Skewers:
   - Preheat your grill to medium-high heat.
   - Place the assembled skewers on the preheated grill.
   - Grill for about 10-12 minutes, turning occasionally, until the chicken is cooked through and the bacon is crispy and caramelized.
   - During the last few minutes of grilling, brush the BBQ sauce over the skewers, turning and brushing occasionally to coat evenly. This will create a sticky and flavorful glaze.
5. Serve:
   - Remove the BBQ chicken skewers with bacon from the grill and transfer to a serving platter.
   - Serve hot, garnished with chopped parsley or green onions if desired.
   - Enjoy your delicious BBQ chicken skewers with bacon!

Tips:

- Bacon Wrapping: Ensure the bacon is wrapped securely around each chicken cube to prevent it from unraveling during grilling.
- Variations: You can add pineapple chunks or bell pepper pieces between the chicken and bacon on the skewers for added flavor and color.

BBQ chicken skewers with bacon are perfect for summer grilling or as a crowd-pleasing appetizer for parties and gatherings. They're easy to make and packed with savory, smoky flavors that everyone will love!

Grilled Lobster Tails

Ingredients:

- 4 lobster tails, thawed if frozen
- 4 tablespoons unsalted butter, melted
- 2 cloves garlic, minced
- 1 tablespoon fresh lemon juice
- Salt and pepper to taste
- Optional: chopped fresh parsley for garnish
- Lemon wedges, for serving

Instructions:

1. Prepare the Lobster Tails:
   - Using kitchen shears, carefully cut through the top shell of each lobster tail lengthwise, stopping at the tail fins. Do not cut through the underside of the tail.
   - Gently spread the shell apart and loosen the meat from the shell, keeping it attached at the base. Lift the lobster meat through the cut shell, resting it on top of the shell.
2. Prepare the Butter Mixture:
   - In a small bowl, combine the melted butter, minced garlic, and fresh lemon juice. Mix well.
3. Preheat the Grill:
   - Preheat your grill to medium-high heat.
4. Season and Grill the Lobster Tails:
   - Season the exposed lobster meat with salt and pepper.
   - Brush the butter mixture generously over the lobster meat and into the shell.
5. Grill the Lobster Tails:
   - Place the prepared lobster tails, shell side down, on the preheated grill.
   - Grill for about 6-8 minutes, depending on the size of the lobster tails, until the meat is opaque and lightly charred on the edges. Baste with the remaining butter mixture during grilling.
6. Serve:
   - Remove the grilled lobster tails from the grill and transfer to a serving platter.
   - Garnish with chopped fresh parsley if desired.
   - Serve hot with lemon wedges on the side.

Tips:

- Grill Temperature: Maintain medium-high heat for even cooking and to prevent overcooking the delicate lobster meat.
- Butter Basting: Basting the lobster tails with the butter mixture during grilling enhances the flavor and keeps the meat moist.

Grilled lobster tails are best served immediately while they are still warm and juicy. They pair wonderfully with a side of melted butter or a fresh green salad for a luxurious meal that's perfect for special occasions or summer gatherings. Enjoy!

BBQ Stuffed Bell Peppers

Ingredients:

- 4 large bell peppers (any color), halved and seeds removed
- 1 pound ground beef or turkey
- 1 small onion, finely chopped
- 2 cloves garlic, minced
- 1 cup cooked rice (white or brown)
- 1 cup barbecue sauce (homemade or store-bought), divided
- 1 cup shredded cheddar cheese (or your favorite cheese), divided
- Salt and pepper to taste
- Optional: chopped fresh parsley or green onions for garnish

Instructions:

1. Preheat the Oven:
    - Preheat your oven to 375°F (190°C).
2. Prepare the Bell Peppers:
    - Cut the bell peppers in half lengthwise and remove the seeds and membranes.
    - Place the pepper halves in a baking dish, cut side up.
3. Cook the Filling:
    - In a large skillet, cook the ground beef or turkey over medium heat until browned and cooked through, breaking it up with a spoon as it cooks.
    - Add the chopped onion and minced garlic to the skillet and cook for 2-3 minutes, until the onion is softened.
4. Assemble the Filling:
    - Stir in the cooked rice, 1/2 cup of barbecue sauce, and 1/2 cup of shredded cheese into the skillet with the meat mixture.
    - Season with salt and pepper to taste. Mix well until combined.
5. Stuff the Peppers:
    - Spoon the barbecue meat mixture evenly into each bell pepper half, pressing down gently to pack the filling.
6. Bake the Stuffed Peppers:
    - Cover the baking dish with foil and bake in the preheated oven for 25-30 minutes, or until the peppers are tender.
7. Add Toppings and Serve:
    - Remove the foil from the baking dish.
    - Drizzle the remaining 1/2 cup of barbecue sauce over the stuffed peppers.
    - Sprinkle the remaining 1/2 cup of shredded cheese over the top.
    - Return the stuffed peppers to the oven, uncovered, and bake for an additional 5-10 minutes, or until the cheese is melted and bubbly.
8. Garnish and Serve:
    - Remove the BBQ stuffed bell peppers from the oven and let them cool slightly.

- Garnish with chopped fresh parsley or green onions if desired.
- Serve hot and enjoy your delicious BBQ stuffed bell peppers!

Tips:

- Variations: You can customize the filling by adding black beans, corn, diced tomatoes, or diced jalapeños for extra flavor and texture.
- Make Ahead: Prepare the stuffed peppers up to step 5, cover tightly with foil, and refrigerate until ready to bake. Increase baking time as needed if baking from cold.

BBQ stuffed bell peppers are a hearty and satisfying meal that's perfect for dinner. They're filled with a delicious blend of barbecue flavors and make a colorful addition to any table. Enjoy!

Grilled Lamb Chops

Ingredients:

- 8 lamb loin chops, about 1 inch thick
- 4 cloves garlic, minced
- 2 tablespoons fresh rosemary leaves, chopped
- 2 tablespoons fresh thyme leaves, chopped
- 1/4 cup olive oil
- Salt and pepper to taste
- Optional: lemon wedges for serving

Instructions:

1. Marinate the Lamb Chops:
    - In a bowl, combine the minced garlic, chopped rosemary, chopped thyme, olive oil, salt, and pepper.
    - Rub the marinade mixture all over the lamb chops, ensuring they are evenly coated.
    - Cover and refrigerate for at least 1 hour, or overnight for maximum flavor.
2. Preheat the Grill:
    - Preheat your grill to medium-high heat. Aim for a temperature of about 400°F (200°C).
3. Grill the Lamb Chops:
    - Remove the lamb chops from the marinade and let any excess marinade drip off.
    - Place the lamb chops on the preheated grill.
    - Grill for about 3-4 minutes per side for medium-rare, or adjust cooking time according to your preference for doneness. Use a meat thermometer to check for an internal temperature of 145°F (63°C) for medium-rare, 160°F (71°C) for medium, or up to 170°F (77°C) for well-done.
4. Rest and Serve:
    - Remove the grilled lamb chops from the grill and let them rest for a few minutes before serving. This allows the juices to redistribute throughout the meat.
5. Optional: Serve with Lemon Wedges:
    - Serve the grilled lamb chops hot, garnished with lemon wedges if desired.

Tips:

- Grilling Time: Cooking time may vary depending on the thickness of the lamb chops and your grill's temperature. Adjust accordingly for desired doneness.
- Internal Temperature: Use a meat thermometer to ensure the lamb chops reach your preferred level of doneness.
- Resting: Allowing the lamb chops to rest after grilling ensures they stay juicy and tender.

Grilled lamb chops are delicious on their own or served with sides like roasted vegetables, couscous, or a fresh salad. They are a wonderful choice for a gourmet meal that's sure to impress! Enjoy your grilled lamb chops straight from the grill with their flavorful marinade and juicy tenderness.

BBQ Tofu

Ingredients:

- 1 block (about 14-16 ounces) firm or extra firm tofu
- 1/2 cup barbecue sauce (homemade or store-bought)
- 2 tablespoons soy sauce or tamari
- 1 tablespoon olive oil or vegetable oil
- 1 tablespoon maple syrup or honey
- 1 teaspoon smoked paprika
- 1/2 teaspoon garlic powder
- Salt and pepper to taste
- Optional: chopped fresh cilantro or green onions for garnish

Instructions:

1. Prepare the Tofu:
   - Drain the tofu and wrap it in paper towels. Place a weight (such as a plate with a heavy can) on top of the tofu to press out excess water for about 15-20 minutes. This step helps the tofu absorb flavors better and achieve a firmer texture.
2. Prepare the Marinade:
   - In a bowl, whisk together the barbecue sauce, soy sauce or tamari, olive oil, maple syrup or honey, smoked paprika, garlic powder, salt, and pepper.
3. Marinate the Tofu:
   - Cut the pressed tofu into slices or cubes, about 1/2-inch to 1-inch thick.
   - Place the tofu pieces in a shallow dish or resealable plastic bag.
   - Pour the marinade over the tofu, ensuring all pieces are well coated. Marinate for at least 30 minutes to 1 hour, or longer for more flavor.
4. Grill the Tofu:
   - Preheat your grill to medium-high heat. If using a stovetop grill pan, preheat it over medium-high heat.
   - Lightly grease the grill grates or grill pan to prevent sticking.
   - Place the marinated tofu pieces on the grill. Grill for about 4-5 minutes on each side, or until grill marks appear and the tofu is heated through, basting with any remaining marinade while grilling.
5. Serve:
   - Remove the grilled BBQ tofu from the grill and transfer to a serving platter.
   - Garnish with chopped fresh cilantro or green onions if desired.
   - Serve hot as a main dish or as part of a meal with your favorite sides.

Tips:

- Tofu Texture: For a firmer texture, you can freeze the tofu before pressing and marinating. Thaw it completely before pressing out the water.

- Grilling Variations: You can also skewer the tofu pieces for BBQ tofu skewers or cut them into smaller cubes for BBQ tofu bites.

BBQ tofu is versatile and pairs well with various sides such as grilled vegetables, rice, quinoa, or a fresh salad. It's a flavorful and healthy option that's sure to satisfy vegetarians and meat-lovers alike. Enjoy your delicious BBQ tofu straight from the grill!

Grilled Avocado

Ingredients:

- 2 ripe avocados
- 1-2 tablespoons olive oil
- Salt and pepper to taste
- Optional toppings: lime wedges, chopped fresh cilantro, diced tomatoes, crumbled feta or goat cheese, a drizzle of balsamic glaze, or hot sauce

Instructions:

1. Prepare the Avocados:
    - Cut the avocados in half lengthwise and remove the pits.
    - Brush the cut sides of the avocados lightly with olive oil to prevent sticking to the grill.
    - Season with salt and pepper to taste.
2. Preheat the Grill:
    - Preheat your grill to medium-high heat.
3. Grill the Avocados:
    - Place the avocado halves cut side down on the preheated grill.
    - Grill for about 2-3 minutes, or until grill marks appear and the avocados are slightly charred.
    - Use a spatula to carefully remove the avocados from the grill.
4. Serve:
    - Transfer the grilled avocados to a serving platter.
    - Squeeze fresh lime juice over the top for added flavor.
    - Add optional toppings such as chopped fresh cilantro, diced tomatoes, crumbled feta or goat cheese, or a drizzle of balsamic glaze or hot sauce for extra flavor and texture.

Tips:

- Choosing Avocados: Make sure to use ripe but firm avocados to ensure they hold up well on the grill.
- Grill Marks: Avoid moving the avocados around too much on the grill to get nice grill marks.
- Extra Flavor: For added flavor, you can marinate the avocados in a bit of lime juice, garlic, and olive oil before grilling.

Grilled avocado is delicious on its own or as part of a larger dish. You can add it to salads, tacos, or enjoy it as a unique side dish. The smoky flavor from the grill enhances the creamy texture of the avocado, making it a delightful addition to your meal. Enjoy!

BBQ Spare Ribs

Ingredients:

- 2 racks of pork spare ribs
- 1/4 cup yellow mustard
- 1/4 cup apple cider vinegar

Dry Rub:

- 1/4 cup brown sugar
- 2 tablespoons paprika
- 1 tablespoon black pepper
- 1 tablespoon salt
- 1 tablespoon chili powder
- 1 tablespoon garlic powder
- 1 tablespoon onion powder
- 1 teaspoon cayenne pepper (optional, for heat)

BBQ Sauce:

- 1 cup barbecue sauce (homemade or store-bought)
- 2 tablespoons honey or brown sugar (optional, for extra sweetness)

Instructions:

1. Prepare the Ribs:
    - Remove the membrane from the back of the ribs. This can be done by sliding a knife under the membrane and then using a paper towel to grip and pull it off.
    - Rinse the ribs under cold water and pat them dry with paper towels.
2. Apply the Mustard and Vinegar:
    - Mix the yellow mustard and apple cider vinegar in a bowl.
    - Rub this mixture all over both sides of the ribs. This helps the dry rub stick and adds flavor.
3. Apply the Dry Rub:
    - In a bowl, combine all the dry rub ingredients.
    - Generously apply the dry rub to both sides of the ribs, pressing it into the meat.
4. Marinate:
    - Wrap the ribs in plastic wrap or place them in a large resealable plastic bag.
    - Refrigerate for at least 2 hours, preferably overnight, to allow the flavors to penetrate the meat.
5. Prepare the Grill:
    - Preheat your grill to 225-250°F (107-121°C) for indirect cooking. If using a charcoal grill, set it up for indirect heat with coals on one side. For a gas grill, turn on one side and leave the other side off.

- Soak some wood chips (hickory, apple, or cherry wood) in water for about 30 minutes and add them to the coals or in a smoker box for the gas grill to add a smoky flavor.
6. Grill the Ribs:
    - Place the ribs on the grill over indirect heat, bone side down.
    - Close the lid and cook the ribs low and slow for about 3-4 hours, or until the meat is tender and pulls away from the bones easily. Maintain a consistent temperature and add more wood chips and coals as needed.
7. Baste with BBQ Sauce:
    - In the last 30 minutes of cooking, baste the ribs with barbecue sauce using a brush. Apply a few coats, allowing the sauce to caramelize and create a sticky glaze.
8. Rest and Serve:
    - Remove the ribs from the grill and let them rest for about 10 minutes.
    - Cut the ribs between the bones into individual pieces.
    - Serve with additional barbecue sauce on the side if desired.

Tips:

- Foil Wrap (Optional): For extra tender ribs, you can wrap the ribs in aluminum foil halfway through the cooking process and return them to the grill. This helps retain moisture. Unwrap them for the last 30 minutes to apply the sauce and allow the ribs to caramelize.
- Check Doneness: The ribs are done when the meat is tender and pulls away from the bones easily. You can also check with a meat thermometer; the internal temperature should be around 190-203°F (88-95°C) for tender ribs.

BBQ spare ribs are a crowd-pleasing dish that's sure to be a hit at your next barbecue. Enjoy the smoky, sweet, and savory flavors of these delicious ribs!

Grilled Caesar Salad

Ingredients:

- 2-3 heads of romaine lettuce, halved lengthwise
- 2 tablespoons olive oil
- Salt and pepper to taste
- 1/2 cup Caesar dressing (homemade or store-bought)
- 1/2 cup grated Parmesan cheese
- 1 cup croutons
- Optional: lemon wedges for serving

Homemade Caesar Dressing (optional):

- 1/2 cup mayonnaise
- 2 tablespoons freshly squeezed lemon juice
- 1 tablespoon Dijon mustard
- 1 tablespoon Worcestershire sauce
- 2 cloves garlic, minced
- 1/4 cup grated Parmesan cheese
- Salt and pepper to taste

Instructions:

1. Prepare the Dressing (if making homemade):
    - In a bowl, whisk together the mayonnaise, lemon juice, Dijon mustard, Worcestershire sauce, minced garlic, and grated Parmesan cheese.
    - Season with salt and pepper to taste. Adjust the consistency with a little water if needed.
    - Set aside.
2. Prepare the Grill:
    - Preheat your grill to medium-high heat.
3. Prepare the Romaine:
    - Rinse the romaine lettuce halves under cold water and pat dry with paper towels.
    - Brush the cut sides of the romaine halves lightly with olive oil.
    - Season with salt and pepper.
4. Grill the Romaine:
    - Place the romaine halves cut side down on the preheated grill.
    - Grill for about 2-3 minutes, or until grill marks appear and the edges are slightly charred. Avoid grilling for too long to keep the lettuce crisp.
    - Use tongs to carefully remove the romaine from the grill and transfer to a serving platter.
5. Assemble the Salad:
    - Drizzle the grilled romaine with Caesar dressing.
    - Sprinkle generously with grated Parmesan cheese.

- Top with croutons.
- Optionally, serve with lemon wedges for squeezing over the salad.

Tips:

- Grilling Time: Keep an eye on the romaine while grilling. The goal is to get a slight char without wilting the lettuce too much.
- Croutons: For extra flavor, you can grill the croutons briefly on the grill as well.
- Additions: Feel free to add grilled chicken, shrimp, or bacon to make the salad more substantial.

Grilled Caesar salad is a unique and flavorful dish that combines the classic elements of Caesar salad with the added depth of grilled lettuce. It's perfect as a starter or a light main course. Enjoy!

BBQ Turkey Burgers

Ingredients:

- 1 pound ground turkey (preferably a mix of dark and light meat for juiciness)
- 1/4 cup finely chopped onion
- 2 cloves garlic, minced
- 1/4 cup breadcrumbs (or panko)
- 1/4 cup barbecue sauce (plus extra for basting)
- 1 tablespoon Worcestershire sauce
- 1 teaspoon smoked paprika
- 1/2 teaspoon salt
- 1/2 teaspoon black pepper
- Olive oil for brushing the grill
- 4 hamburger buns
- Optional toppings: lettuce, tomato, red onion, pickles, cheese, avocado, etc.

Instructions:

1. Prepare the Grill:
    - Preheat your grill to medium-high heat.
    - Brush the grill grates with olive oil to prevent sticking.
2. Make the Turkey Burger Patties:
    - In a large bowl, combine the ground turkey, chopped onion, minced garlic, breadcrumbs, 1/4 cup barbecue sauce, Worcestershire sauce, smoked paprika, salt, and pepper.
    - Mix until all ingredients are well combined, but do not overmix to avoid tough burgers.
    - Divide the mixture into 4 equal portions and shape each portion into a patty about 3/4-inch thick. Make a small indentation in the center of each patty to prevent them from puffing up during grilling.
3. Grill the Turkey Burgers:
    - Place the turkey burgers on the preheated grill.
    - Grill for about 5-6 minutes per side, or until the internal temperature reaches 165°F (74°C) as measured with a meat thermometer.
    - During the last couple of minutes of grilling, brush each burger with additional barbecue sauce and let it caramelize slightly.
4. Toast the Buns:
    - If desired, place the hamburger buns cut side down on the grill for 1-2 minutes, or until lightly toasted.
5. Assemble the Burgers:
    - Place each grilled turkey burger on the bottom half of a toasted bun.
    - Add your favorite toppings such as lettuce, tomato, red onion, pickles, cheese, avocado, etc.

- Top with the other half of the bun.
6. Serve:
    - Serve the BBQ turkey burgers hot with additional barbecue sauce on the side if desired.

Tips:

- Moisture: To keep turkey burgers juicy, avoid using 100% lean ground turkey; a mix of dark and light meat works best.
- Resting Time: Let the turkey burgers rest for a few minutes after grilling to retain their juices.
- Flavor Variations: Add different spices or herbs to the burger mixture, such as cumin, oregano, or fresh parsley, to vary the flavor.

BBQ turkey burgers are a tasty and lighter option for your next barbecue, packed with smoky and savory flavors that everyone will enjoy. Serve them with your favorite sides like coleslaw, sweet potato fries, or a fresh salad. Enjoy!

Grilled Oysters

Ingredients:

- 1 dozen fresh oysters in their shells
- 4 tablespoons unsalted butter, softened
- 2 cloves garlic, minced
- 1 tablespoon fresh parsley, finely chopped
- 1 tablespoon lemon juice
- 1 teaspoon hot sauce (optional)
- Salt and pepper to taste
- Lemon wedges for serving

Instructions:

1. Prepare the Butter Mixture:
   - In a small bowl, mix together the softened butter, minced garlic, chopped parsley, lemon juice, hot sauce (if using), salt, and pepper until well combined.
2. Preheat the Grill:
   - Preheat your grill to high heat.
3. Prepare the Oysters:
   - Scrub the oyster shells under cold water to remove any dirt or debris.
   - Carefully shuck the oysters, keeping the oyster meat in the bottom shell and discarding the top shell. Be cautious of any sharp edges and use an oyster knife if you have one.
4. Grill the Oysters:
   - Place the shucked oysters on the half shell directly on the hot grill.
   - Spoon a small amount of the butter mixture onto each oyster.
   - Close the grill lid and cook for about 5-7 minutes, or until the oysters are plump and the butter is bubbly and slightly browned.
5. Serve:
   - Carefully remove the oysters from the grill using tongs, as they will be very hot.
   - Arrange the grilled oysters on a platter.
   - Serve immediately with lemon wedges on the side for squeezing over the top.

Tips:

- Shucking Oysters: If you're not comfortable shucking oysters, you can ask your fishmonger to do it for you. Alternatively, you can place the oysters on the grill unshucked until they just start to open, then remove and shuck them carefully.
- Flavor Variations: Experiment with different butter mixtures, such as adding finely chopped shallots, chives, or a splash of white wine.
- Serving Ideas: Grilled oysters pair well with crusty bread to soak up the delicious juices, a fresh green salad, or as part of a seafood platter.

Grilled oysters are a fantastic appetizer or main course for seafood lovers, offering a unique and flavorful way to enjoy fresh oysters with minimal preparation. Enjoy the smoky, garlicky goodness of grilled oysters at your next barbecue or special occasion!

BBQ Pulled Chicken

Ingredients:

- 2 pounds boneless, skinless chicken breasts or thighs (or a combination)
- 1 cup barbecue sauce (homemade or store-bought)
- 1/2 cup chicken broth
- 1/4 cup apple cider vinegar
- 1 tablespoon brown sugar
- 1 tablespoon Worcestershire sauce
- 1 teaspoon smoked paprika
- 1 teaspoon garlic powder
- 1 teaspoon onion powder
- 1/2 teaspoon salt
- 1/2 teaspoon black pepper
- Optional: extra barbecue sauce for serving

Instructions:

1. Prepare the Chicken:
   - In a bowl, mix together the barbecue sauce, chicken broth, apple cider vinegar, brown sugar, Worcestershire sauce, smoked paprika, garlic powder, onion powder, salt, and pepper.
2. Cook the Chicken:
   - Slow Cooker Method:
     - Place the chicken in the slow cooker.
     - Pour the sauce mixture over the chicken, ensuring it's well-coated.
     - Cook on low for 6-7 hours or on high for 3-4 hours, until the chicken is tender and easily shredded with a fork.
   - Instant Pot Method:
     - Place the chicken in the Instant Pot.
     - Pour the sauce mixture over the chicken, ensuring it's well-coated.
     - Close the lid and set the valve to sealing.
     - Cook on high pressure for 10 minutes, then let the pressure release naturally for 10 minutes before doing a quick release.
   - Oven Method:
     - Preheat your oven to 325°F (163°C).
     - Place the chicken in a baking dish and pour the sauce mixture over the chicken, ensuring it's well-coated.
     - Cover the dish with foil and bake for 1.5-2 hours, or until the chicken is tender and easily shredded with a fork.
3. Shred the Chicken:
   - Remove the chicken from the cooking liquid and shred it using two forks.

- Return the shredded chicken to the slow cooker, Instant Pot, or baking dish and mix it with the remaining sauce.
4. Serve:
    - Serve the BBQ pulled chicken on sandwich buns, over rice, in tacos, or as desired.
    - Optionally, drizzle with extra barbecue sauce if desired.

Tips:

- Additions: You can add finely chopped onions or bell peppers to the cooking liquid for extra flavor.
- Storage: Store any leftovers in an airtight container in the refrigerator for up to 4 days or freeze for up to 3 months.
- Serving Ideas: Serve with coleslaw, pickles, or potato salad for a complete meal.

BBQ pulled chicken is a crowd-pleasing dish that's easy to prepare and perfect for any occasion. Enjoy its tender, flavorful goodness in a variety of ways!

Grilled Sweet Potatoes

Ingredients:

- 3-4 medium sweet potatoes
- 2-3 tablespoons olive oil
- 1 teaspoon salt
- 1/2 teaspoon black pepper
- 1 teaspoon smoked paprika (optional)
- 1 teaspoon garlic powder (optional)
- Fresh herbs for garnish (optional, such as parsley or cilantro)

Instructions:

1. Prepare the Sweet Potatoes:
   - Wash and peel the sweet potatoes.
   - Cut them into 1/2-inch thick slices or wedges.
2. Parboil the Sweet Potatoes:
   - Bring a large pot of water to a boil.
   - Add the sweet potato slices and boil for about 5 minutes until they are just starting to become tender but are still firm enough to hold their shape.
   - Drain the sweet potatoes and let them cool slightly.
3. Preheat the Grill:
   - Preheat your grill to medium-high heat.
4. Season the Sweet Potatoes:
   - In a large bowl, toss the sweet potato slices with olive oil, salt, pepper, smoked paprika, and garlic powder until evenly coated.
5. Grill the Sweet Potatoes:
   - Place the sweet potato slices on the preheated grill.
   - Grill for about 3-5 minutes per side, or until grill marks appear and the potatoes are tender and slightly charred.
   - Be sure to turn them carefully with a spatula to avoid breaking them.
6. Serve:
   - Remove the grilled sweet potatoes from the grill and transfer them to a serving platter.
   - Garnish with fresh herbs if desired.

Tips:

- Consistency: Parboiling the sweet potatoes helps ensure they cook evenly on the grill and stay tender without burning.
- Flavor Variations: Try adding other spices such as cumin, chili powder, or cinnamon for different flavor profiles.

- Dips: Serve with a dipping sauce such as aioli, ranch dressing, or a yogurt-based sauce for added flavor.

Grilled sweet potatoes are a versatile and tasty addition to any meal. They pair well with a variety of main dishes and can be enjoyed by themselves as a healthy snack. Enjoy the sweet, smoky flavors of grilled sweet potatoes!

BBQ Brisket

Ingredients:

- 1 whole beef brisket (8-10 pounds), untrimmed
- 1/4 cup yellow mustard (for coating)

Dry Rub:

- 1/4 cup brown sugar
- 1/4 cup paprika
- 2 tablespoons coarse salt
- 2 tablespoons black pepper
- 2 tablespoons chili powder
- 1 tablespoon garlic powder
- 1 tablespoon onion powder
- 1 teaspoon cayenne pepper (optional, for heat)
- 1 teaspoon ground cumin

Spritz (optional, to keep the brisket moist during smoking):

- 1 cup apple juice or apple cider vinegar
- 1 cup water

BBQ Sauce (optional, for serving):

- 1 cup barbecue sauce (homemade or store-bought)

Instructions:

1. Prepare the Brisket:
    - Rinse the brisket under cold water and pat it dry with paper towels.
    - Trim excess fat from the brisket, leaving about 1/4 inch of fat to keep the meat moist during cooking.
2. Apply the Mustard and Dry Rub:
    - Rub the entire brisket with yellow mustard to help the dry rub adhere.
    - In a bowl, combine all the dry rub ingredients.
    - Generously coat the brisket with the dry rub, pressing it into the meat on all sides.
3. Preheat the Smoker or Grill:
    - Preheat your smoker or grill to 225-250°F (107-121°C) for indirect cooking.
    - Add wood chips or chunks (such as hickory, oak, or mesquite) to the smoker for a smoky flavor.
4. Smoke the Brisket:
    - Place the brisket on the smoker or grill, fat side up.

- Close the lid and smoke the brisket for about 1.5 hours per pound, maintaining a consistent temperature.
    - Every hour or so, spritz the brisket with the apple juice and water mixture to keep it moist (optional).
5. Wrap the Brisket (Texas Crutch, optional):
    - When the internal temperature of the brisket reaches about 165°F (74°C), wrap the brisket tightly in aluminum foil or butcher paper to help it cook faster and stay moist.
    - Continue smoking until the internal temperature reaches 195-205°F (90-96°C).
6. Rest the Brisket:
    - Remove the wrapped brisket from the smoker and let it rest for at least 1 hour in a cooler or warm oven to allow the juices to redistribute.
7. Slice and Serve:
    - Carefully unwrap the brisket and transfer it to a cutting board.
    - Slice the brisket against the grain into 1/4-inch thick slices.
    - Serve with barbecue sauce on the side if desired.

Tips:

- Monitoring Temperature: Use a meat thermometer to monitor the internal temperature of the brisket accurately.
- Patience: Smoking a brisket takes time and patience. Avoid rushing the process to achieve the best results.
- Resting: Letting the brisket rest is crucial for a juicy and tender final product.

BBQ brisket is a true labor of love that rewards you with rich, smoky flavors and tender meat. It's perfect for special occasions, gatherings, or any time you want to treat yourself to some delicious barbecue. Enjoy!

Grilled Eggplant Parmesan

Ingredients:

- 2 large eggplants, sliced into 1/2-inch thick rounds
- Olive oil for brushing
- Salt and pepper to taste
- 2 cups marinara sauce (homemade or store-bought)
- 2 cups shredded mozzarella cheese
- 1 cup grated Parmesan cheese
- Fresh basil leaves for garnish

Optional Breading (for a slightly more traditional texture):

- 1 cup breadcrumbs
- 1/2 cup grated Parmesan cheese
- 1 teaspoon dried Italian seasoning
- 2 eggs, beaten

Instructions:

1. Prepare the Eggplant:
   - Lay the eggplant slices on a baking sheet.
   - Sprinkle both sides with salt and let them sit for about 30 minutes to draw out excess moisture.
   - Rinse the eggplant slices under cold water and pat them dry with paper towels.
2. Optional Breading (Skip if you prefer not to bread the eggplant):
   - In a bowl, mix the breadcrumbs, grated Parmesan cheese, and Italian seasoning.
   - Dip each eggplant slice in the beaten eggs, then coat with the breadcrumb mixture.
   - Set the breaded slices aside on a baking sheet.
3. Preheat the Grill:
   - Preheat your grill to medium-high heat.
4. Grill the Eggplant:
   - Brush the eggplant slices (whether breaded or not) with olive oil on both sides.
   - Season with salt and pepper.
   - Place the eggplant slices on the preheated grill.
   - Grill for about 4-5 minutes per side, or until they are tender and have nice grill marks.
   - Remove from the grill and set aside.
5. Assemble the Eggplant Parmesan:
   - Preheat your oven to 375°F (190°C).
   - In a large baking dish, spread a thin layer of marinara sauce on the bottom.
   - Arrange a layer of grilled eggplant slices over the sauce.

- Spoon some marinara sauce over the eggplant, then sprinkle with shredded mozzarella and grated Parmesan cheese.
- Repeat the layers until all the eggplant is used, finishing with a layer of sauce and cheese on top.
6. Bake the Dish:
    - Cover the baking dish with aluminum foil.
    - Bake in the preheated oven for about 20 minutes.
    - Remove the foil and bake for an additional 10-15 minutes, or until the cheese is bubbly and golden brown.
7. Serve:
    - Let the Grilled Eggplant Parmesan cool for a few minutes before serving.
    - Garnish with fresh basil leaves.
    - Serve hot with a side of pasta, a green salad, or crusty bread.

Tips:

- Drawing Out Moisture: Salting the eggplant slices helps to reduce bitterness and moisture, leading to a better texture when grilled.
- Homemade Marinara Sauce: For extra flavor, make your own marinara sauce with fresh tomatoes, garlic, olive oil, and herbs.
- Grill Marks: Ensure your grill is well-oiled to prevent the eggplant from sticking and to get those beautiful grill marks.

Grilled Eggplant Parmesan is a delicious and healthy twist on a beloved classic, perfect for summer meals and gatherings. Enjoy the smoky, cheesy goodness of this dish!

BBQ Salmon

Ingredients:

- 4 salmon fillets (6-8 ounces each), skin-on or skinless
- Olive oil, for brushing
- Salt and pepper, to taste
- Lemon wedges, for serving
- Fresh herbs (optional, for garnish)

BBQ Sauce:

- 1/2 cup barbecue sauce (homemade or store-bought)
- 2 tablespoons soy sauce or tamari
- 2 tablespoons honey or maple syrup
- 1 tablespoon Dijon mustard
- 1 tablespoon apple cider vinegar
- 2 cloves garlic, minced
- 1 teaspoon smoked paprika
- 1/2 teaspoon ground cumin
- Salt and pepper, to taste

Instructions:

1. Prepare the BBQ Sauce:
    - In a small bowl, whisk together all the BBQ sauce ingredients until well combined. Set aside.
2. Prepare the Salmon:
    - Pat the salmon fillets dry with paper towels.
    - Brush both sides of the salmon fillets lightly with olive oil.
    - Season with salt and pepper to taste.
3. Preheat the Grill:
    - Preheat your grill to medium-high heat.
4. Grill the Salmon:
    - Place the salmon fillets on the preheated grill, skin-side down if they have skin.
    - Close the grill lid and cook for about 4-6 minutes, depending on the thickness of the fillets.
    - Carefully flip the salmon fillets using a spatula and brush the tops with the prepared BBQ sauce.
    - Close the grill lid again and cook for another 4-6 minutes, or until the salmon is cooked through and flakes easily with a fork.
    - Optionally, brush more BBQ sauce on the salmon during the last minute of cooking for extra flavor.
5. Serve:
    - Remove the grilled BBQ salmon from the grill and transfer to a serving platter.

- Garnish with fresh herbs and lemon wedges.
- Serve hot with additional BBQ sauce on the side if desired.

Tips:

- **Grill Temperature:** Maintain a medium-high heat to ensure the salmon cooks evenly without burning.
- **Flavor Variations:** Customize the BBQ sauce by adjusting the sweetness or spiciness to your preference. Add a pinch of cayenne pepper for heat or a squeeze of fresh lemon juice for brightness.
- **Salmon Doneness:** Salmon is cooked when it reaches an internal temperature of 145°F (63°C) or until the flesh flakes easily with a fork.

BBQ salmon is a nutritious and flavorful dish that's quick and easy to prepare on the grill. It's perfect for summer gatherings or a weeknight dinner. Enjoy the smoky, sweet, and tangy flavors of BBQ salmon!

Grilled Sausage and Peppers

Ingredients:

- 1 package (about 4-6 links) Italian sausage (sweet or hot, pork or chicken)
- 2-3 bell peppers (red, yellow, and/or green), seeded and sliced into strips
- 1 large onion, sliced
- 2-3 tablespoons olive oil
- Salt and pepper, to taste
- 1 teaspoon dried oregano (optional)
- 1 teaspoon dried basil (optional)
- Fresh parsley or basil leaves, chopped (for garnish)
- Hoagie rolls or crusty bread (optional, for serving)

Instructions:

1. Prepare the Sausage and Peppers:
    - Preheat your grill to medium-high heat.
2. Grill the Sausage:
    - Place the sausage links on the preheated grill.
    - Grill for about 15-20 minutes, turning occasionally, until the sausages are browned and cooked through with an internal temperature of 160°F (71°C) for pork sausage or 165°F (74°C) for chicken sausage.
3. Grill the Peppers and Onions:
    - While the sausages are grilling, toss the sliced bell peppers and onions with olive oil, salt, pepper, dried oregano, and dried basil in a bowl until evenly coated.
    - Place the seasoned peppers and onions in a grill basket or directly on the grill grate.
    - Grill for about 10-15 minutes, stirring occasionally, until the peppers and onions are tender and slightly charred.
4. Assemble the Dish:
    - Once the sausages are cooked through, remove them from the grill and let them rest for a few minutes.
    - Slice the sausages into diagonal pieces.
    - Arrange the grilled sausage slices, peppers, and onions on a serving platter.
    - Garnish with chopped fresh parsley or basil.
5. Serve:
    - Serve the grilled sausage and peppers hot, either on their own or in hoagie rolls or crusty bread for sandwiches.

Tips:

- Grill Preparation: Ensure your grill grates are clean and well-oiled to prevent sticking.

- Variations: Feel free to add other vegetables such as zucchini or mushrooms to the grill along with the peppers and onions.
- Serving Ideas: Serve with marinara sauce for dipping, or a side of pasta or salad.

Grilled sausage and peppers is a versatile dish that's perfect for a casual weeknight dinner or a backyard barbecue. Enjoy the smoky flavors and hearty combination of sausage and grilled vegetables!

BBQ Pork Chops

Ingredients:

- 4 pork chops, about 1 inch thick (bone-in or boneless)
- Salt and pepper, to taste
- 1 cup barbecue sauce (homemade or store-bought)
- 2 tablespoons olive oil

Instructions:

1. Prepare the Pork Chops:
   - Preheat your grill to medium-high heat.
2. Season the Pork Chops:
   - Pat the pork chops dry with paper towels.
   - Season both sides of the pork chops with salt and pepper.
3. Grill the Pork Chops:
   - Brush the pork chops with olive oil to prevent sticking and help them achieve nice grill marks.
   - Place the pork chops on the preheated grill.
   - Grill for about 4-5 minutes per side, depending on the thickness of the chops, or until they reach an internal temperature of 145°F (63°C) for medium rare, or up to 160°F (71°C) for well done.
4. Apply the BBQ Sauce:
   - During the last few minutes of grilling, brush both sides of the pork chops generously with barbecue sauce.
   - Continue to grill for another 1-2 minutes per side, brushing with more sauce as desired, until the sauce caramelizes slightly and the pork chops are fully cooked through.
5. Rest and Serve:
   - Remove the pork chops from the grill and let them rest for a few minutes before serving.
   - Serve hot with additional barbecue sauce on the side if desired.

Tips:

- Grill Temperature: Maintain medium-high heat for a nicely seared exterior while keeping the inside juicy.
- Internal Temperature: Use a meat thermometer to ensure the pork chops reach a safe internal temperature of at least 145°F (63°C) for medium rare or up to 160°F (71°C) for well done.
- Flavor Variations: Customize the barbecue sauce by adding ingredients like garlic powder, smoked paprika, or a dash of hot sauce for extra flavor.

Grilled BBQ pork chops are a simple and delicious way to enjoy pork on the grill. They pair well with classic barbecue sides like cornbread, coleslaw, or grilled vegetables. Enjoy the smoky, tangy flavors of BBQ pork chops at your next cookout!

Grilled Caesar Salad

Ingredients:

- 2 heads of romaine lettuce, halved lengthwise
- Olive oil, for brushing
- Salt and pepper, to taste
- Caesar dressing (homemade or store-bought)
- Grated Parmesan cheese, for garnish
- Croutons (optional), for serving

Instructions:

1. Prepare the Grill:
    - Preheat your grill to medium-high heat.
2. Prepare the Romaine Lettuce:
    - Cut the romaine lettuce heads in half lengthwise, keeping the core intact to hold the leaves together.
3. Grill the Romaine Lettuce:
    - Brush the cut sides of the romaine lettuce halves with olive oil.
    - Season with salt and pepper to taste.
    - Place the lettuce halves, cut side down, on the preheated grill.
    - Grill for about 2-3 minutes, or until grill marks appear and the lettuce starts to char slightly. The outer leaves will wilt slightly while the core remains crisp.
4. Assemble the Salad:
    - Remove the grilled romaine lettuce halves from the grill and place them on a serving platter or individual plates, cut side up.
    - Drizzle Caesar dressing generously over each grilled lettuce half.
5. Serve:
    - Garnish with grated Parmesan cheese and croutons if desired.
    - Serve immediately while the lettuce is still warm.

Tips:

- Grill Temperature: Ensure your grill is well-heated to quickly sear the romaine lettuce and achieve nice grill marks.
- Dressing: Use your favorite Caesar dressing, whether homemade or store-bought. The smoky flavor from grilling pairs wonderfully with the creamy and tangy Caesar dressing.
- Variations: Add grilled chicken, shrimp, or salmon to turn the salad into a complete meal.

Grilled Caesar salad is a refreshing and flavorful dish that makes a great appetizer or side for any summer meal or barbecue. Enjoy the unique combination of grilled flavors and classic Caesar salad elements!

BBQ Chicken Quesadillas

Ingredients:

- 2 cups cooked chicken, shredded or diced (you can use leftover grilled or roasted chicken)
- 1/2 cup barbecue sauce (homemade or store-bought)
- 4 large flour tortillas
- 2 cups shredded cheese (cheddar, Monterey Jack, or a blend)
- 1/2 cup diced red onion (optional)
- 1/4 cup chopped fresh cilantro (optional)
- Olive oil or butter, for cooking

Instructions:

1. Prepare the BBQ Chicken:
   - In a bowl, toss the cooked chicken with barbecue sauce until evenly coated. Adjust the amount of sauce to your preference.
2. Assemble the Quesadillas:
   - Lay out two tortillas on a clean surface.
   - Sprinkle half of the shredded cheese evenly over each tortilla.
   - Divide the BBQ chicken mixture evenly over the cheese on each tortilla.
   - If using, sprinkle diced red onion and chopped cilantro evenly over the chicken.
3. Top and Cook:
   - Sprinkle the remaining shredded cheese evenly over the chicken mixture on each tortilla.
   - Place the remaining tortillas on top to cover the filling, creating two quesadillas.
4. Cook the Quesadillas:
   - Heat a large skillet or griddle over medium heat.
   - Lightly brush one side of each quesadilla with olive oil or spread with butter.
   - Carefully place the quesadillas, oiled/buttered side down, in the skillet.
   - Cook for about 3-4 minutes on each side, or until the tortillas are golden brown and crispy, and the cheese is melted and gooey.
5. Serve:
   - Remove the quesadillas from the skillet and place them on a cutting board.
   - Let them rest for a minute or two before slicing each quesadilla into wedges.
   - Serve hot with additional barbecue sauce or sour cream on the side for dipping.

Tips:

- Chicken: Use pre-cooked chicken for quicker preparation, such as leftover grilled chicken, rotisserie chicken, or even canned chicken.
- Cheese: Experiment with different types of cheese to suit your taste preferences.

- Variations: Add sliced jalapeños, diced bell peppers, or black beans for extra flavor and texture.

BBQ chicken quesadillas make for a fantastic meal or snack, perfect for a quick lunch or dinner. Enjoy the savory, smoky flavors wrapped in warm, crispy tortillas!

Grilled Ratatouille

Ingredients:

- 1 large eggplant, sliced into 1/2-inch rounds
- 2 medium zucchini, sliced lengthwise into 1/2-inch thick strips
- 2 medium yellow squash, sliced lengthwise into 1/2-inch thick strips
- 2 bell peppers (red, yellow, or orange), halved and seeded
- 2 tomatoes, sliced into 1/2-inch rounds
- 1 red onion, sliced into thick rings
- 4 cloves garlic, minced
- 1/4 cup olive oil
- Salt and pepper, to taste
- 2 tablespoons balsamic vinegar (optional)
- Fresh herbs (such as basil or thyme), chopped, for garnish

Instructions:

1. Preheat the Grill:
    - Preheat your grill to medium-high heat.
2. Prepare the Vegetables:
    - In a large bowl, toss the sliced eggplant, zucchini, yellow squash, bell peppers, tomatoes, and red onion with olive oil, minced garlic, salt, and pepper until evenly coated.
3. Grill the Vegetables:
    - Place the vegetables on the preheated grill in a single layer or use a grill basket for smaller pieces.
    - Grill the vegetables for about 3-5 minutes per side, or until they are tender and have grill marks. Cook time may vary depending on the thickness of the vegetables.
4. Assemble the Ratatouille:
    - Once grilled, remove the vegetables from the grill and let them cool slightly.
    - Arrange the grilled vegetables in an overlapping pattern on a serving platter or in a baking dish.
    - Drizzle with balsamic vinegar if using.
    - Season with additional salt and pepper to taste.
5. Serve:
    - Garnish the grilled ratatouille with chopped fresh herbs, such as basil or thyme.
    - Serve warm or at room temperature as a side dish or main course.

Tips:

- Grill Preparation: Ensure your grill grates are clean and lightly oiled to prevent sticking.

- Vegetable Variations: Feel free to add or substitute other vegetables such as mushrooms, asparagus, or cherry tomatoes.
- Storage: Grilled ratatouille can be stored in an airtight container in the refrigerator for up to 3-4 days. It can be served cold, at room temperature, or reheated gently before serving.

Grilled ratatouille is a versatile dish that highlights the vibrant flavors of summer vegetables. It's perfect for serving alongside grilled meats or as a vegetarian main dish. Enjoy the smoky goodness of grilled vegetables in this delicious ratatouille!

BBQ Beef Brisket Sandwiches

Ingredients:

- 1 beef brisket (3-4 pounds), trimmed of excess fat
- Salt and pepper, to taste
- 1 tablespoon smoked paprika
- 1 tablespoon garlic powder
- 1 tablespoon onion powder
- 1 tablespoon brown sugar
- 1 teaspoon cayenne pepper (adjust to taste)
- 1 cup beef broth or water
- 1 cup barbecue sauce (homemade or store-bought)
- Hamburger buns or sandwich rolls, for serving
- Coleslaw (optional), for topping

Instructions:

1. Prepare the Brisket:
    - Preheat your smoker or grill to 225-250°F (107-121°C) for indirect cooking.
    - In a small bowl, combine smoked paprika, garlic powder, onion powder, brown sugar, cayenne pepper, salt, and pepper to create a dry rub.
2. Season and Smoke the Brisket:
    - Season the brisket generously on all sides with the dry rub mixture, pressing it into the meat.
    - Place the brisket on the smoker or grill, fat side up.
    - Close the lid and smoke the brisket for about 1.5 to 2 hours per pound, or until the internal temperature reaches about 200-205°F (93-96°C) and the meat is tender and easily pulls apart.
3. Wrap and Rest:
    - If desired, wrap the brisket in aluminum foil or butcher paper when it reaches an internal temperature of about 165°F (74°C) to help retain moisture.
    - Let the wrapped brisket rest for at least 30 minutes to 1 hour to allow the juices to redistribute.
4. Prepare the BBQ Sauce:
    - In a small saucepan, heat the barbecue sauce over low heat until warmed through.
5. Slice and Assemble the Sandwiches:
    - Slice the brisket thinly against the grain.
    - Pile the sliced brisket onto hamburger buns or sandwich rolls.
    - Drizzle with warm barbecue sauce.
    - Optionally, top with coleslaw for added crunch and flavor.
6. Serve:
    - Serve the BBQ beef brisket sandwiches immediately while warm.

Tips:

- Choosing Brisket: Look for a brisket with good marbling for tenderness and flavor.
- Resting Time: Allowing the brisket to rest after smoking is crucial for juicy and flavorful meat.
- Storage: Leftover brisket can be stored in the refrigerator for 3-4 days or frozen for up to 2-3 months. Reheat gently in the oven or microwave before serving.

BBQ beef brisket sandwiches are a crowd-pleasing favorite, perfect for gatherings, parties, or a satisfying family meal. Enjoy the rich, smoky flavors and tender beef in every bite!

Grilled Fajitas

Ingredients:

- 1.5 pounds flank steak or chicken breasts/thighs, sliced into thin strips
- 3 bell peppers (red, green, and yellow), seeded and sliced
- 1 large onion, sliced
- 2 tablespoons olive oil
- Juice of 1 lime
- 3 cloves garlic, minced
- 1 tablespoon chili powder
- 1 teaspoon ground cumin
- 1 teaspoon paprika
- 1/2 teaspoon dried oregano
- Salt and pepper, to taste
- Tortillas (flour or corn), for serving
- Optional toppings: shredded cheese, sour cream, guacamole, salsa, chopped cilantro, lime wedges

Instructions:

1. Marinate the Meat:
    - In a bowl, combine the olive oil, lime juice, minced garlic, chili powder, ground cumin, paprika, dried oregano, salt, and pepper.
    - Add the sliced steak or chicken to the marinade, making sure to coat all pieces evenly. Cover and refrigerate for at least 30 minutes, or up to 2 hours.
2. Prepare the Vegetables:
    - In a separate bowl, toss the sliced bell peppers and onions with 1 tablespoon of olive oil, salt, and pepper.
3. Preheat the Grill:
    - Preheat your grill to medium-high heat.
4. Grill the Meat and Vegetables:
    - Remove the meat from the marinade and discard the marinade.
    - Place the marinated meat on the preheated grill. Cook for 4-5 minutes per side for steak (or until desired doneness) or 5-6 minutes per side for chicken (or until cooked through).
    - Remove the meat from the grill and let it rest for a few minutes before slicing thinly against the grain.
    - Meanwhile, grill the bell peppers and onions in a grill basket or directly on the grill grates, stirring occasionally, until they are tender and slightly charred, about 8-10 minutes.
5. Assemble the Fajitas:
    - Warm the tortillas on the grill for about 20-30 seconds per side, or until heated through and lightly charred.

- Place some sliced grilled meat and grilled vegetables onto each tortilla.
- Serve with optional toppings such as shredded cheese, sour cream, guacamole, salsa, chopped cilantro, and lime wedges.
6. Serve:
    - Roll up the tortillas and serve immediately while warm.

Tips:

- Slicing Meat: For tender fajitas, slice the meat thinly against the grain.
- Variations: You can use shrimp or tofu instead of steak or chicken for a seafood or vegetarian option.
- Make-Ahead Tip: You can marinate the meat and prepare the vegetables ahead of time, making it a great option for easy entertaining.

Grilled fajitas are a versatile and delicious meal that everyone will enjoy. The combination of grilled meat, flavorful vegetables, and toppings creates a satisfying and customizable dish perfect for any occasion!

BBQ Stuffed Zucchini Boats

Ingredients:

- 4 medium zucchini
- 1 tablespoon olive oil
- Salt and pepper, to taste
- 1 cup cooked quinoa or rice
- 1 cup cooked black beans (canned, rinsed and drained)
- 1 cup corn kernels (fresh, frozen, or canned)
- 1/2 cup diced bell peppers (any color)
- 1/2 cup diced red onion
- 1/2 cup barbecue sauce (homemade or store-bought)
- 1/2 cup shredded cheese (cheddar, Monterey Jack, or a blend)
- Fresh cilantro or parsley, chopped, for garnish (optional)

Instructions:

1. Prepare the Zucchini:
    - Preheat your grill to medium-high heat.
    - Cut each zucchini in half lengthwise. Use a spoon to scoop out the seeds and create a hollow "boat". Leave about 1/2 inch of flesh inside the zucchini halves.
    - Brush the cut sides of the zucchini boats with olive oil and season with salt and pepper.
2. Grill the Zucchini Boats:
    - Place the prepared zucchini boats cut side down on the preheated grill.
    - Grill for about 4-5 minutes, or until the zucchini is slightly charred and just tender. Remove from the grill and set aside.
3. Prepare the Filling:
    - In a large bowl, combine cooked quinoa or rice, black beans, corn kernels, diced bell peppers, diced red onion, and barbecue sauce. Mix well to combine.
4. Assemble the Stuffed Zucchini Boats:
    - Spoon the filling mixture evenly into the grilled zucchini boats, pressing gently to pack the filling.
    - Sprinkle shredded cheese over the top of each stuffed zucchini boat.
5. Grill the Stuffed Zucchini Boats:
    - Place the stuffed zucchini boats back on the grill, close the lid, and grill for another 5-7 minutes, or until the filling is heated through and the cheese is melted and bubbly.
6. Serve:
    - Remove the stuffed zucchini boats from the grill and garnish with chopped fresh cilantro or parsley, if desired.
    - Serve hot as a main dish or side dish.

Tips:

- Variations: Feel free to customize the filling with your favorite vegetables, beans, or grains.
- Make-Ahead: You can prepare the filling ahead of time and assemble the stuffed zucchini boats just before grilling.
- Vegetarian/Vegan Options: Omit the cheese or use a dairy-free cheese alternative for a vegan version.

BBQ stuffed zucchini boats are a flavorful and nutritious dish that's sure to please everyone at your next barbecue or summer gathering. Enjoy the smoky flavors and hearty textures of this delicious grilled dish!

Grilled Banana S'more

Ingredients:

- Ripe bananas, peeled and sliced lengthwise
- Chocolate chips or chocolate bars, broken into pieces
- Marshmallows
- Graham crackers, crushed (optional, for serving)

Instructions:

1. Prepare the Grill:
    - Preheat your grill to medium-high heat.
2. Assemble the Banana S'mores:
    - Place the banana slices on a cutting board or plate, cut side up.
    - Sprinkle chocolate chips or place pieces of chocolate on top of half of the banana slices.
3. Add Marshmallows:
    - Place marshmallows on top of the chocolate layer.
4. Assemble the S'mores:
    - Create banana "sandwiches" by placing another banana slice, cut side down, on top of each marshmallow-topped slice to form a sandwich.
5. Grill the Banana S'mores:
    - Carefully place the assembled banana s'mores on the preheated grill.
    - Grill for about 2-3 minutes per side, or until the bananas are softened, chocolate is melted, and marshmallows are toasted and gooey.
6. Serve:
    - Remove the grilled banana s'mores from the grill and transfer them to a serving plate.
    - Optionally, sprinkle crushed graham crackers over the top for extra crunch and flavor.
    - Serve immediately while warm and gooey.

Tips:

- Grill Preparation: Use a grill basket or aluminum foil to prevent the banana s'mores from sticking to the grill grates.
- Variations: Experiment with different chocolate flavors, such as dark chocolate or flavored chocolate bars.
- Toppings: Serve with a dollop of whipped cream or a scoop of vanilla ice cream for an extra indulgent treat.

Grilled banana s'mores are a fun and delicious dessert that combines the sweetness of bananas, chocolate, and gooey marshmallows with a hint of smokiness from the grill. Enjoy this delightful twist on a classic camping favorite!

www.ingramcontent.com/pod-product-compliance
Lightning Source LLC
LaVergne TN
LVHW062047070526
838201LV00080B/2110